INDIA

MAURITIUS • RÉUNION • SEYCHELLES
COMORO ISLANDS AND MAYOTTE
MADAGASCAR

Contents

CREOLE ABCs

Achards — Mixture of finely chopped and marinated vegetables.

Avalasse — Heavy rain.

Bas — The coast.

Bazardier — Peddler.

Bichiques — Elvers (baby eels).

Boucan — Hut.

Brèdes — Leaves of various vegetables prepared like spinach.

Cachalot — Sugar-cane lorry (literally, "whale").

Cafre — Black.

Case — House.

Chatini — Chutney.

Charlatan — Madagascan witch doctor.

Chouchou — Vegetable with edible root and leaves.

Creole — Refers to people born in the islands; in local parlance, islanders with African ancestry.

Fangan — Tree fern.

Filao — Casuarina, large tree resembling a pine.

Habitation — Plantation house.

Hauts — Mountain (Réunion).

Ilet — Mountain hamlet.

Malabar — Tamil.

Marine — Landing stage.

Marmaille — Child.

Marron — Maroon, fugitive slave.

Multipliant — Banyan.

Rempart — Cliff.

Rhum arrangé — Rum flavoured with exotic fruit.

Tamarind — A kind of acacia.

Vacoa — Pandanus.

Varangue — Verandah.

Z'arabe — Muslim.

Z'oreille — Frenchman from the "Métropole" – France.

Zourites — Octopus.

MAURITIUS

Exuberantly Creole

Mauritius is the sugar-cane island of the Indian Ocean. Fields of cane cultivation, broken only by small villages, stretch over a wide plateau above the tropical white sand beaches, breezy bays and glorious seascapes.

It was also the island of the dodo, a large, flightless bird whose good-natured simplicity resulted in the poor creature's total extinction.

The island forms part of the Mascarene Archipelago, all that remains of an ancient land mass which once united Asia and Africa. To the southwest lies Réunion Island, with its savagely beautiful volcanic landscape, while some 560 km (350 miles) east appears Rodrigues Island, a mere dot in the ocean, surrounded by even smaller islets and reefs, and an integral part of Mauritius.

Small as Mauritius is, covering only 1,865 sq km (720 sq miles), it is one of the more densely populated places in the world and supports over 1.2 million people, most of them descendants of Indians brought in to work the sugar plantations after the abolition of slavery. There's also a large Chinese community and a number of Creoles, descended from French colonists. Africans and Malagasy add to the mixture of races and religions, one happy result being that there's nearly always a festival going on in one of the numerous Hindu or Chinese temples, mosques or Christian churches.

On the jittery world market of today, sugar is an uneasy staple commodity. Increasing tourism partially helps to counteract unemployment and low incomes: a good airport, magical beaches and the flowery loveliness of the resorts beckon visitors in ever greater numbers. Inland, mountains rise in lonely splendour and you may glimpse a Java deer vanishing into the bushes. Bamboo thickets, lagoons, plunging waterfalls and delicately pretty Creole buildings are all part of the Mauritian scene.

In the 19th century the French writer Bernardin de Saint-Pierre used this island as the setting for his idyllic and tragic romance of two love-struck adolescents, *Paul et Virginie*. The novel helped usher in the Romantic movement. Mauritius knew its most glittering moments in the middle years of the 19th century. Joseph Conrad and Mark Twain both dropped by at different times. Baudelaire visited for three weeks, and wrote of a port filled with masts and sails and air haunted by the

MAURITIUS

Île aux Serpents

Île Ronde

Île Plate

Ilot Gabriel

INDIAN OCEAN

Coin de Mire

C. Malheureux

Pereybere

Pointe aux cannoniers

Mont Choisy ☆ Grand Baie

Fond du sac

Île d'Ambre

Trou aux Biches ☆

Goodlands

Triolet

Poudre d'or

Mapou

Baie du Tombeau

Pamplemousses

Rivière du Rempart

Belle Vue Maurel

Roches Noires

Pointe Lafayette

Montagne Longue

L'Aventure

Plaines des Roches

Pointe de Flacq

PORT LOUIS

La Nicolière

Domaine des Pailles ☆ Le Pouce
▲ 812m

Pieter Both
▲ 823 m

Centre de Flacq

Belle Mare

Moka

St. Pierre

R. du Poste de Flacq

Palmar

Pte Quatre Cocos

Beau Bassin

Le Réduit ☆

Quartier Militaire

Trou d'eau douce

Bambous

La Ferme

Rose Hill

Bel Air

Touessrok

Médine

Quatre Bornes

Île aux Cerfs

Flic en Flac ☆

Casela Bird Park

Phoenix

Montagne Blanche

Grande Rivière Sud-Est

Vacoas

Trou aux cerfs ☆

Curepipe

Mont Lagrave
638 m

Grande Rivière Sud-Est

Montagnes Bambous

Ilot Flamants

La Preneuse ☆

Tamarin

Tamarind Falls

Mare aux Vacoas

Domaine du Chasseur

de la Grande ière Noire

Rivière Noire

Plaine Champagne

Nouvelle France

Rose Belle

Riche en Eau

ux Bénitiers

▲ 828 m

Piton de la Petite R. Noire

Cratère Kanaka

Rivière du Poste

Plaine Magnien

Mahébourg

Île aux Aigrettes

Le Morne Brabant

Chamarel

Mont Cocotte
▲ 771 m

Savanne

Union Vale ✈

Blue Bay

-Ouest t Fourneau

Bel Ombre

Chemin Grenier

Rochester Falls

Rivière des Anguilles

L'Escalier

Baie du Cap

Surinam

Souillac

Bénarès

N

Le Gris Gris

0   10 km

scent of green tamarinds. Darwin, naturally, couldn't resist this naturalist's paradise, and the *HMS Beagle* put in here on her famous voyage. Seen from grey, drizzly Europe, it appeared like a dream of rare flowers, foaming cascades, airy colonial houses and balmy days.

Independent since 1968, Mauritius is hard at work now keeping down its population growth and pushing up its income. The friendly inhabitants of all the rainbow of races will confide their problems but will also express their optimism in the progress being achieved by their welcoming Indian Ocean homeland. For Mauritius has a fascinating past, an inviting present and a rosy future.

A Brief History

16th century	The Portuguese drop anchor in 1502. One of their names for the island is Cisne ("swan"). They do not settle. The Dutch visit in 1598 and take possession.
17th century	Mauritius, as the island is named, in honour of Holland's Stadtholder Prince Maurice of Nassau, is a useful stopping-point for ships on their way to Dutch bases in Java. Attempts at agriculture on Mauritius fail.
18th century	The French assume control in 1715 and change the name to Ile de France. Six years later their first colonists arrive. Slaves are brought in to work the sugar plantations and to man naval vessels. Mahé de La Bourdonnais, Governor from 1735 to 1747, establishes the first sugar factory.
19th century	The island has become a key spot in the Indian Ocean. The British find this irresistible, particularly during the Napoleonic Wars, since it is close to the brightest jewel in their imperial crown—India. They take over in 1810 (more officially in 1814 at the Treaty of Paris) and, having re-established the name Mauritius or Maurice Island, attempt to apply British traditions and the English language. The inhabitants accede politely but continue speaking their Creole tongue and leading a French lifestyle. In 1835, abolition of slavery is finally imposed, and slave owners are paid off by Britain. Asian workers are brought in to provide cheap labour. Sugar is king in the 1850s, while in literature and in real life, Mauritius is at the height of fashion. But the opening of the Suez Canal (1869) isolates it

8

from shipping routes. The island suffers a series of disasters, including cyclones and epidemics. By the end of the century Mauritius is falling into decline.

20th century–present

During World War II, Mauritius is a British naval and air base. In 1968, the island becomes an independent member of the British Commonwealth, then a Republic in 1992. Sugar remains the chief crop, but tourism becomes a mainstay of the economy.

Sightseeing

Port Louis

The island capital was named after France's Louis XV. It's a busy place and the little harbour has an important, wide-awake look. Shaded by palms and dotted with statues of local worthies, **Place d'Armes** is the town's main square linking the seafront to imposing **Government House**, the oldest building in Mauritius. It was built in 1738 in colonial style for Mahé de La Bourdonnais, the island's most illustrious governor. He is commemorated by a statue near the waterfront, a diplomatic step away from the regal figure of Queen Victoria. Other buildings round the square, such as the municipal theatre, are reminders of colonial times.

Pope Hennessy Street contains some lovely Creole buildings and leads to the **Champ de Mars** where there is animated horse-racing Saturdays from May to mid-December. This race track was originally laid out by the French in 1740 as a military parade ground. Opposite stands a **Chinese Pagoda**, one of several in the town.

Local culture is promoted by the Mauritius Institute. Its **Natural History Museum** on Chaussée Street merits a visit for its displays including a stuffed specimen of the much lamented dodo.

St Louis' Catholic Cathedral gives on to a square with an attractive fountain dating from 1786 and a statue of the 13th-century French saint-king. A discreet distance away is **St James's Anglican Cathedral**, looking as though it has been transplanted from a 19th-century English village. You can almost hear the virtuous rustle of bonnets. In spite of its seemly aspect, the cathedral is actually built over an old powder magazine, hence the name of the street, Rue de la Poudrière.

To pay tribute to the islanders' tolerant religious and racial views, you will also want to see the green and white **Jummah** 9

PORT-LOUIS

Benarès St. · Dr. H. Sakir St. · Calcutta St. · Madras St.

Dr. Edgar Laurent St. · Dr. Edgar Laurent St.

Monseigneur Leen Av. · Dr. Ulislam Society St. · Madame Caretan St. · Boulevard de la Concorde

La Paix St. · Hatch St. · Inkerman St. · La Paix St. · Sebastopol St. · Shakespeare St.

La Paix Stream · La Paix St. · Diore St. · Sebastopol St.

La Citadelle

Fort Adélaïde

Pagode chinoise

Mausolée du Comte de Malartic

Champ de Mars

Dr. Eugène Laurent St. · Dr. Eugène Laurent St.

Seneevassen St. · Arsenal St. · Dauphine St. · St. Virgil St. · St. Georges St. · Dr. Eugène Laurent St. · Suffren St. · Mgr Gonin St. · Pope Hennessy St. · D'Estaing St. · Frère Félix de Valois St.

Dr. Sun Yat Sen St. · Anquetil St. · Rivière St. · Olier St. · Remy Ollier St. · Dr. Eugène Laurent St. · Church St. · Descroizilles St. · Sookdeo Bissoondoyal St. · Yishnu Kchettr

Mosquée Jummah

Quartier Chinois

Royal Road · Emmanuel St. · Hormann St. · Jummah Mosque St. · Bourbon St. · Newton St. · Jules Koenig St. · St. Louis St. · Quibri St. · Poudrière St. · St. Denis St. · Seetulsing St.

Dr. Joseph St. · Farquhar St. · L. Pasteur St. · Jules Koenig St. · Malartic St. · Poudrière St.

Cathédrale St-Louis

Théâtre municipal

Hôtel de Ville

Cour Suprême

Cathédrale St-James

Champ de Lort St.

Hôtel du Gouvernement

Mauritius Institute

Jardin de la Compagnie des Indes

Musée de la Photographie

Corderie St. · Sir William Newton St. · Intendance St. · Chaussée St. · Sir C. Antelme St. · Edith Cavell St. · Poivre St. · St. Louis St. · St-George St. · Desforges St. · Dr. Rouget St. · D'Artois St.

Marché central

Duke of Edinburgh Av. · Queen Elisabeth Av. · Chevreau St. · Sir S. Ramgoolam St. · Volcy Pougnet St. · Mère Barthélemy St. · Tennay St. · Rémy St.

Rogers House

Place d'Armes

Église Immaculée Conception

Grand Baie · M2

Immigration Square

Musée de la Poste

Poste centrale

Louis St. · President J. Kennedy St. · Barracks St. · Chevreau St.

Port

New Quay St. · Raoul St. · Victoria Square · Lord Kitchener St. · Deschartres St.

Caserne centrale

Olivia St. · La Galère St. · Alan Frank Wen St. · Entrecasteaux St. · Monseigneur Leen Av.

N ←

0   100   200 m
0   100   200 yd

Bassin Caudan · Rose-Hill Curepipe · M2

Mosque on Royal Road, with and moulded friezes on the walls and finely worked doors. A fair distance away in the same direction (too far to walk), the **Indo-Tamil Temple** is ornate and multi-domed, contrasting with the barren peaks behind.

The lively and colourful **central covered market** is near the mosque on both sides of Farquhar Street and is open daily to about 5 p.m. Each section has its own speciality: luscious fruit and vegetables piled up in baskets, fish and meat, spices and souvenirs.

A trip up to the monument Marie Reine de la Paix on **Signal Hill**, where wealthier citizens live, lays Port Louis at your feet.

Domaine Les Pailles, a short distance from Port Louis, is a tourists' dream, with a wide range of interesting attractions and facilities. Here, visitors have a unique opportunity to learn about the old way of life. In a magnificent natural setting, you can see a reconstructed old sugar mill powered by an ox, and alembic or rum-making still. You can also enjoy a pleasant few hours wandering idly around the estate, visiting its spice garden, or meandering in horse-drawn carriages through pleasant valleys. There's also a miniature train, and excursions are organized in four-wheel drive vehicles to a nature reserve with birds, deer and monkeys on the domain's outskirts.

As Dead as a Dodo

The dodo was too nice to survive. Unique to Mauritius, this flightless bird was so tame that it was child's play to shoot it. Idle soldiers and sailors gleefully used it as target practice. In an almost unique instance of wantonly killing for the sake of killing, man quite deliberately exterminated the bird; it was not even good to eat.

The dodo was described by a Dutch seaman, Jacob Cornelis Van Neck, in his Voyage to the East Indies (1598–1601) as: "a bird bigger than a swan, with no feathers on its body which is covered by a black fluff;...on its back it has the same number of feathers as it has years...; in place of wings, it has similar feathers, black and turned back. It has no tongue, a curved beak, tall, scaly legs with only three claws on each foot..."

Soon after that, references (and birds) got fewer and fewer, till today we're left with a few reconstructed specimens in museums throughout the world. But the dodo lives on in memories, on stamps, coats-of-arms and in common parlance as something totally and utterly extinct.

Around the Island

A good motorway cuts across the Central Plateau, making the journey between the capital Port Louis, on the west coast, and Mahébourg, on the east side, easy and comfortable. Another main road circles the island, affording wonderful views of sea and shoreline and passing through coastal resorts. Smaller, picturesque roads also wander inland to extinct volcanoes, lakes and botanical gardens.

North Coast

This is the most touristic part of Mauritius, stretching between Port Louis and Cap Malheureux, at the tip of the island.

Pamplemousses lies 11 km (7 miles) north of St Louis. The village surrounds the **church of St Francis of Assisi**, the oldest on the island (1756). But Pamplemousses is mostly famous for its **Botanical Gardens**, begun in 1735 when Mahé de La Bourdonnais bought the property. From 1767, the French Intendant Pierre Poivre was responsible for planting trees and flowers on the land. Today the gardens are reduced to a quarter their original size but their loveliness has only increased with time. They boast more than 500 species including the talipot palm that takes from 30 to 80 years to flower then promptly dies. Floating like bluish-green trays in a rectangular pond are huge *Victoria regia* water-lilies, some of the leaves measuring 150 cm (almost 5 ft) across.

The wrought-iron entrance gates date from the middle of the 19th century. Inside, a marble column is inscribed with the names of the botanists and generous donators who contributed towards the gardens. Grand, ancient trees establish royal dominion over a well-kept lawn that sweeps to the Château de Mon Plaisir, a colonial mansion built by the English in the 19th century. Palms, some 200 years old, border the alleys.

If you go to **Trou aux Biches**, look out for the lovely Hindu temple at Triolet and visit the excellent Aquarium with 200 types of fish, live coral, and fascinating exhibits, wonderfully presented.

At **Mont Choisy**, one of the most popular beaches on the island, shaded by casuarinas, you'll find perfect safe bathing with plenty of windsurfing and sailing possibilities. From here onwards lie some of the island's most inviting beaches gleaming with powdery white sand, sheltered from the wind and protected by a coral reef perfect for underwater exploration. One of the most splendid resorts—and the most renowned—is **Grand Baie**, the centre for many sea-related activities. In Grand Baie itself, visit the local gallery with interesting exhibitions by Mauritian artists, next to the colourful Tamil temple.

Nearby **Péreybère**, with its lovely clear blue waters, is another paradise for swimmers. At the very far north is **Cap Malheureux**, which supposedly got its name from the fact that it was the spot where the English landed in 1810 to conquer the island. On a calm day there's a wonderful view out to sea, especially of the volcanic island of **Coin de Mire** with its massive, plunging cliffs. Do not miss the lovely little church in the village of Cap Malheureux.

The Centre

The interior spreads north of the road linking Port Louis and Mahébourg. It's the sugar-cane region, composed of the cool central plateau and the lowlands close to the coast.

Instead of taking the motorway, follow the old "Royal Road" *(Route royale)* from Port Louis to Curepipe and Mahébourg. You first come to **Beau Bassin**. Here the **Balfour Gardens**, situated at the edge of a gorge, provide a pleasant and instructive interlude. Darwin stayed for a few days in the nearby white manor house after landing from the *HMS Beagle*.

Rose Hill is one of the few towns on Mauritius with an English-sounding name. Its chief claim to fame, apart from a wide range of cultural activities, is a handsome town hall and an old theatre. A short drive north of Rose Hill lies the **Château de Réduit**, a magnificent colonial mansion surrounded by tropical gardens. It was built in 1748 by the French governor Barthélemy David as a country residence and refuge for women and children of the French East India Company in case Port Louis should be attacked by the English. Later it was enlarged and remodeled as residence of the successive French and British governors, and today it is the official residence of the President (and closed to the public).

Not far away, at the foot of the Ory Mountains, lies the gracious old Creole house called **Eureka**, built at the beginning of the 19th century out of indigenous woods. The story goes that when the son of the Mauritian Judge of the High Court bought the house at auction, he shouted "Eureka" when his bid was accepted and the word stuck. His descendants have transformed part of the house into a museum.

13

In the middle of the island lies the island's principal residential town, **Curepipe** (meaning pipe cleaner), a delightful, relatively cool place 550 m (1,804 ft) above sea level where the temperatures all year round are lower than on the coast. Today Curepipe's population numbers 60,000, including the elite of Franco-Mauritian society. The town began to prosper at the end of the 19th century when the inhabitants of Port Louis fled from a plague of malaria that had struck the capital. The **statue** in front of the colonial-style town hall commemorates the ill-fated love of Paul and Virginie, described in Bernardin de Saint-Pierre's novel. Curepipe's botanical garden is smaller than that of Pamplemousses: take a leisurely stroll through it to admire the tropical vegetation. The town offers some of the best shopping on the island, notably for model boats (particularly beneath the arcades).

Before leaving Curepipe, most tourists visit the **Trou aux Cerfs** (Deer's Hole), just out of town. It's the forested crater, 300 m (985 ft) wide and 100 m (325 ft) deep, of an extinct volcano, with a pond on the bottom. From the road circling the summit there are some magnificent panoramas over practically the whole island: fields of sugar cane rolling down to the sea, and a mountain chain to the south. When the weather is fine you might just catch a glimpse of Réunion island floating like a purple cloud on the horizon 160 km (100 miles) away.

You'll discover another facet of the island if you leave the urban district near Port Louis and travel towards the north coast. Far from the resorts, scattered in villages and hamlets among the fields of sugar cane, the islanders lead a nonchalant, appealing way of life.

East Coast

The former Royal Road leads straight to **Mahébourg**. It's a bustling little fishing and commercial town. Because it lies off the usual tourist route, it has been able to maintain a more traditional, more authentic Mauritian atmosphere than Port Louis. You can spend a pleasant few hours wandering round town and investigating the shops in the centre. At the entrance to the town, the **Naval Museum** tells the story of the Battle of Grand Port. In the 18th-century French colonial-style mansion housing the museum, the French and British commanders, Duperré and Willoughby, both wounded in the course of the battle, were treated side by side. They ended by shaking hands, ushering in an *entente cordiale*. The museum also displays furniture and objects that belonged to Governor Mahé de la Bourdonnais, a series of engravings relating the island's colonial history, and a collection of postage stamps.

From Mahébourg, a short road leads through flowers and trees, past the resort of Pointe d'Esny and a row of luxurious villas, to **Blue Bay**, surrounded by a semi-circle of casuarina trees. The beach here is often considered one of the best on the island because of its deep, clear blue waters—an ideal bay for water sports of all kinds.

The bay of **Vieux Grand Port**, where the Dutch first landed in 1598, is just to the north of Mahébourg. It was also in these waters, in 1810, that Napoleon's navy beat the British (who got their revenge on land four months later). A few reminders of that era remain scattered here and there—like the cannon pointing their barrels out to sea at Pointe du Diable.

Beyond Anse Jonchée, a vast area has been set aside for the **Domaine du Chasseur** (also called the Domaine des Grands Bois), a magnificent nature and hunting reserve where deer, monkeys and wild boar live in the heart of a lush tropical forest containing a whole selection of interesting botanical specimens to delight the naturalist and hiker. Eucalyptus, ebony, wild orchids, bergamots, palms and cinnamon trees grow in profusion. Local birds once in danger of extinction have been successfully reintroduced here, such as the Mauritius kestrel, which plunges down suddenly onto little rodents, its favourite prey.

In a similar vein, nearby **Le Val Nature Park** is located in the heart of a valley, surrounded by lush vegetation. You can see carp, freshwater fish, shrimp, and prawns bred in chemically treated water, as well as birds, deer and monkeys.

Excellent beaches abound on the east coast. **Belle Mare** has its addicts, drawn to its magnificent sweep of beach stretching from the little fishing village of Trou d'Eau Douce to the Pointe de Flacq. Further north lies **Roches Noires**, black rocks and pale sand, much appreciated in summer because of the constant sea breezes and the excellent fishing.

Further south, the **Ile aux Cerfs**, a 20-minute crossing by small boat or catamaran from Touessrok, has deer roaming wild. It is one of the most popular excursions in Mauritius. The beaches and lagoon are perfect for bathing.   15

The South

The south coast is the most rugged, the most hilly and without doubt the most beautiful. Strangely, it is less popular with visitors.

South of Port Louis, the small town with the delightful name of **Flic en Flac** provides an excellent example of the cosmopolitan mood of the island and boasts a typical beach with gentle white sand fringed by casuarina trees. Its lagoon is ideal for snorkelling.

A short distance away, nearly 2,000 birds of 150 varieties call the **Casela Bird Park** home. Some of them, for example the star-of-the-show Pink Pigeon, have narrowly escaped extinction. There are also tortoises (a Mauritian speciality), monkeys, ostriches and even a tiger. Orchids bloom, in season.

Tamarind trees grow in abundance along the west coast and gave their name to **Tamarin**, a clean and pleasant little resort with a fabulous beach (one of the most popular with Mauritians), that also has the island's main salt flats. Thanks to its huge breakers it has also become a surfer's paradise.

In the extreme southwest corner of Mauritius, Le Morne Peninsula is topped by a flat mountain, **Le Morne Brabant**, 556 m (1,824 ft) high, so difficult to reach that it once served as a hideout for runaway slaves. At sea level, the beaches and underwater life around the peninsula are superb. It is also a good place for fishing, in particular for marlin. Shell-collectors should not miss the **Shellorama**, just before you reach Le Morne. Ostensibly a shop, it also has a museum displaying an extensive collection of bewitching shells from the Indian Ocean and elsewhere.

Between Morne Brabant and Mahébourg, the coast is wild and rugged. As far as Souillac, the road follows the ocean, passing through tiny hamlets of painted huts nestling at the foot of mountains whose summits are wreathed in clouds of mist. Now and then, a deserted little creek will beckon you to go down for a swim.

Souillac, the main town of southern Mauritius, was named after François Vicomte de Souillac, governor of the island from 1779 to 1787. The backdrop of the Savanne Mountains makes a handsome setting. To see the vegetation of the area, flourishing despite frequent cyclones, visit the **Telfair Gardens**, with their gigantic Indian almond trees and banyans. For a little culture, call in at Le Nef, the house-cum-museum of the Mauritian poet Robert Edward

Hart, who lived in this cottage until his death in 1954. It is partly built of coral and stands high on the cliff sculpted by the waves, with a striking view of the coastline.

For an invigorating whiff of sea air, go to the cliffs at **Gris-Gris**, east of Souillac and the furthest point south on the island. The beach is dangerous, but fishermen obstinately go out laying lobster and crayfish pots.

Another curiosity nearby is the **Vanille Crocodile Farm**, near the large village of Rivière des Anguilles in a wild spot of tropical rain forest. Brought in from Madagascar, the reptiles have settled happily on Mauritius and increased dramatically from the single male and four females originally imported. The site has also become a popular tourist attraction, and children (and their parents, too) love the mad medley of monkeys, bats and wild pigs, among other adorable animals which also include the giant Telfair lizard.

Just outside Souillac, navigate your way through the labyrinthine fields of sugar-cane to reach the **Rochester Falls**, where the waters have carved the basalt into curious, mostly upright shapes. The cascade crashes down from about 10 m (33 ft) above.

From the southwestern tip of the island, two forested roads lead up to **Chamarel**. Apart from offering superb views, the region is famous for its **Terres de Couleurs**, coloured earths brought about by the erosion of volcanic ash. Test tubes of samples in a rainbow of hues can be bought from freelance vendors or from the local shops. The best time to visit the area is at dawn. The colours—violet, blue, purple, red, green, brown and yellow—never fade despite tropical rainfall, and for geologists in particular this lunar landscape is fascinating. Nearby, the dramatic **Chamarel Falls** stand in total contrast to that landscape, with rich vegetation and humid air.

While coffee is produced in the Chamarel region, the area surrounding **Grand Bassin** is planted with tea. But Grand Bassin is known mainly for its lake, slumbering in the crater of an extinct volcano. At 702 m (2,300 ft) above sea level, the site is totally eerie. In the centre lies a tiny island. Hindus flock here in February to celebrate Maha Shivaratree in the temples along the banks and throw offerings of flowers into the sacred lake.

The road between Chamarel and Grand-Bassin goes through **Plaine-Champagne**, apparently 17 named for its creamy white privet flowers that look like froth on a glass of bubbly. At an altitude of 720 m (2,363 ft), this is part of a national park, affording a wonderful view down over the wooded slopes of the **Black River Gorges**. This is good hiking country; you can follow a path along the river to reach the gorges, noted for the variety of birds and vegetation unique to the island.

Energetic hikers might also like to tackle the **Kanaka Crater**. This extinct volcano can only be reached by rough tracks through tea plantations.

Rodrigues

A brilliant blue lagoon holds Rodrigues in its embrace. This tiny scrap of an island, far to the east of Mauritius, is a place where time takes on another meaning, a place to daydream.

The capital, **Port Mathurin**, is a little colonial town made up of half a dozen streets, lined with Chinese boutiques, handicraft shops, restaurants, wooden Creole houses and some grand old administrative buildings—the finest is the **Commissariat**, dating from 1873. Get up early on Saturday to enjoy the colour and excitement of the **market**. In the mornings, the town is always lively and wide awake, but from 3 p.m. it starts to snooze, and by 8 p.m. it's fast asleep. Highlight of the week is the arrival of *Mauritius Pride,* a cargo boat linking Port Louis and Port Mathurin in 36 hours.

To explore the island, you can hire a jeep or four-wheel drive, a mini-moke or bicycle. The roads are practically deserted, winding through fields of corn and manioc, potatoes and pimentos. Visit the little villages to meet the Creole people, ever eager to make friends: **Mount Lubin**, affording a view of the whole island, **Saint Gabriel** with its stone-built church, Malabar, Citronnelle, Quatre-Vents. Don't miss **Port Sud-Est**, a fishing village where you can watch the women digging for *zourites* (a local octopus) in the muddy bed of the lagoon.

The island's best beach is at **Pointe Coton**, a vast stretch of white sand, but there are other good places for swimming or sunbathing at Trou d'Argent, spectacularly sited between two cliffs, Baladirou, Anse Ali, Pâté Reynieux, Graviers, and Fumier. And to really get away from it all, take a boat trip from Port-Mathurin to l'Ile aux Cocos or its neighbour l'Ile aux Sables, both superb **nature reserves** with fabulous beaches and thousands of sea birds.

Rodrigues has two natural wonders: at **Caverne Patate** in

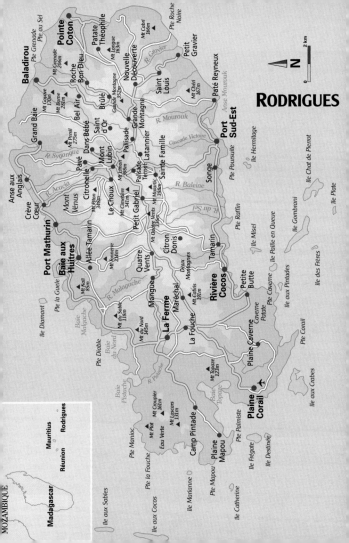

the south a guide with an oil lamp will take you into the subterranean depths to view eerie formations of stalagmites and stalactites. Between Plaine Coral and Anse Guitor, great cliffs of **coral** are quarried like marble: watch the men sawing off huge chunks of rock that will be cut into bricks for building.

Dining Out

The resorts offer fine French, international and modern cuisine. Chinese, Indian and Creole provide further variety.

Mutton, chicken, fish, seafood and vegetables are offered in delicious curry sauces. Dishes are accompanied by rice and, usually, *achards,* a variety of vegetable chutneys, and perhaps pickled limes. A favourite dish is millionaire's salad, made from hearts of palm. Fish and seafood or freshwater crayfish provide local flavour. Smoked marlin is an island delicacy.

Imported wines are expensive, but local wine (made from imported grape juice) is appreciated by many, as are the island-brewed beers.

Shopping

Curepipe is the most reputed spot for tourist shopping but Port Louis is quite good as well.

Chinese and Indian merchants will dazzle you with sari lengths in shimmering silk or cotton. Hand-woven saris and blouses are the most attractive. Shirts, dresses and even knitwear are likely to be better bargains than back home.

Baskets, hats, fans, table napkins and tablemats provide inexpensive souvenirs of island handicrafts. Along with a whole range of shell jewellery and ornaments, there are objects in wood and jade. Straw figurines, dolls and macramé complete a particularly varied range of local handicrafts.

Models of boats and old sailing ships are often exquisitely 21 made. Numerous excellent craftsmen in Curepipe compete for attention. Duty-free goods include cameras, watches —and diamonds. Bargaining is not likely to get you very far. Each town will have its *boutik,* a little local shop stocking everything, but there are plenty of super-markets, too.

Practical Information

Climate. The heat is never unbearable. The rainy season is between the end of November and March. On the plateau it's 19°C (66°F) on average in August and 25°C (77°F) in February; it's warmer on the coast. Rodrigues has a very dry climate.

Clothing. Casual, preferably cotton for comfort, plus a jacket or wrap for the evening. Dress with reasonable reticence in the towns. Discreet clothing is required for visits to mosques and Hindu temples.

Credit Cards. The major credit cards are accepted everywhere.

Currency. The Mauritius *rupee* (R or MUR) is divided into 100 *cents* (or *sous*). Coins range from 5 cents to 10 R, banknotes from 25 to 2000 R.

Electricity. The current is 220/240 V, and the plugs are like those used in the UK, with three flat prongs.

Driving. In Mauritius vehicles drive on the *left*, as in the UK.

Hours. In Port Louis, shops are open Monday to Friday 9 a.m.–5 p.m., on Saturdays until noon. In Curepipe they open Monday to Saturday 9 a.m.–6 p.m., closing on Thursdays at noon; they may also open on Sunday mornings. Banks are open Monday to Thursday 9.15 a.m.–3.15 p.m., a bit longer on Fridays, and on Saturdays 9.30–11.30 a.m. Post offices are open Monday to Friday 9–11 a.m. and 12–4 p.m., on Saturdays 9–11 a.m.

Language. English is the official language, French is commonly spoken, and everyone uses Creole (derived from French).

Passport. Visitors in possession of a passport valid for a further 6 months at minimum and a return ticket may stay up to six months. Visas are not required for nationals of EU countries and Switzerland, or holders of Canadian or American passports.

Time. GMT + 4.

Tipping. 10% in hotels and restaurants.

Vaccinations. Certificates of vaccination against cholera and yellow fever are only required of visitors travelling from infected areas.

RÉUNION .

Far-Flung France

The fragrance of the tamarind trees alone would entice many a Parisian to this unlikely-looking and unforgettable corner of France. Further tempt him with emerald-green lagoons, mighty mountains and refreshing waterfalls, graceful people and a sense of tropical timelessness, and the Parisian might decide never to leave.

Réunion, westernmost of the Mascarene Islands, rises up out of a bed of volcanic lava in the Indian Ocean some 800 km (500 miles) east of Madagascar. A French Overseas Department, it has a multiracial population numbering 766,000. With an area of 2,512 sq km (970 sq miles), it's about the size of Luxembourg. Inviting green coastal forests border a mountainous interior, where three immense volcanic craters have formed lush valley basins, or *cirques*. A still-seething volcano, La Fournaise, literally The Furnace, provides a breathtaking backdrop, and from time to time it pours forth a river of lava to add an extra bit to the island's area. And several other rugged peaks cluster round the island's summit, Piton des Neiges, the Snow Pinnacle, reaching an altitude of more than 3,000 m (10,000 ft).

A veritable spider's web of roads curling in from all sides enables you to explore much more of Réunion's awesome interior than the man who discovered the island nearly five centuries ago, Admiral Pedro de Mascarenhas. (The Mascarene islands—the trio of Réunion, Mauritius and Rodrigues—were named after him.) A good highway circumnavigates the island and there are even stretches of motorway. But despite this, not much has changed. A round trip of the island—it can be covered in a day—reveals an immense and undisturbed tropical garden that provides much of the inspiration for today's perfume industry. Geraniums, gladioli, begonias, dahlias and asters can all be found blooming wild under the plane trees, palms and fruit trees next to orchids and other more exotic flowers. The only problem is the occasional cyclone that roars in with winds of 300 km (185 miles) an hour, ripping through the plantations and unroofing houses. Fortunately, modern forecasting techniques give plenty of warning when it's time to batten down the windows.

You can see the influence of religion over the years in the names of communities, every other one dedicated to a saint. But this is deceptive in today's

24

melting-pot. Many islanders go to church but also worship in the Tamil temple, or practise black magic.

At one time, around 80 per cent of Réunion's population were slaves from Madagascar and Africa working on the coffee and sugar plantations. Since then, the island has become a meeting point for many cultures, even if the atmosphere is as French as croissants and café au lait. The people are colourfully diverse—Europeans (in Creole z'Oreilles), Africans (Cafres), Tamil Indians (Malabars), Muslim Indians (z'Arabes) and other Asians. They send senators and deputies to represent them in the French parliament. Many work in the island's only industries: sugar-processing and rum-making.

A Brief History

16th century   The island is discovered by the Portuguese navigator Pedro de Mascarenhas in 1513, but methodical colonization begins much later.

17th century   In 1638 France takes possession of the island, soon to be named Bourbon to please the king. The first settlers belatedly arrive in 1646—a dozen mutineers exiled from Madagascar. The outcasts' life is easy amidst the tropical bounty. The first voluntary colonists reach Réunion in 1663.

18th century   Saint-Denis becomes the capital. The King of France buys the isle of Bourbon from the French East India Company in 1764. Agriculture is diversified, with spices complementing the cultivation of coffee. The island takes the name La Réunion in 1793.

19th century   With Napoleon in power in Paris, the island's name is changed to Bonaparte. British troops occupy the island from 1810 to 1815. An uprising by slaves in Saint-Leu is suppressed. The cultivation of sugar cane begins in 1820, requiring intense manpower and leading to the importation of thousands of slaves. In 1841, with the discovery of artificial insemination of vanilla, the island becomes the world's principal supplier. Slavery is abolished in 1848. Réunion recruits workers in India. The "coffee era" ends in 1867. In 1880 the first Chinese arrive from Canton. From 1895 onwards, perfume plant cultures (geraniums, vetiver and ylang-ylang) are laid out.

25

| 20th century–present | In World War I Réunion sends 14,000 soldiers to fight in Europe; 3,000 are killed. Blockaded in World War II, the island suffers hunger and hardship. On March 19, 1946, Réunion becomes a French Overseas Department. Vast public works projects are undertaken, but unemployment remains a serious problem. |

Sightseeing

Réunion cannot be called a beachy island, though the west coast has 27 km (17 miles) of appealing sand beaches of all colours. Most of the perimeter of the island is a harsh conjunction of land and sea, spectacular to look at but not really the tropical coast of your holiday dreams. Many of the top attractions are inland, and upland, in the volcanic mountains and the brave villages scattered among them. Our survey begins on the north coast in the island's lively, mostly modern capital city of more than 145,000 inhabitants, surrounded on three sides by steep mountains.

Saint-Denis

Administrative power has been centred in Saint-Denis since the days of the French East India Company. It became the official capital of the island in 1738. It has been the Prefecture of the Réunion *département* since 1946. The streets, set out at right angles, bring a sense of order, and it is easy to find your way around. Most of the interesting sights are on or around the main street, avenue de la Victoire.

At the avenue's waterfront end, **Le Barichois** brings to mind the port that was once there. With its promenade, gardens and ancient cannon, it is the focus of attraction for the locals, particularly in the evening. One of the finest buildings in the neighbourhood is the **Préfecture**, in a garden shaded by trees a century old. It long served as the office of the Compagnie des Indes. At the time, this splendid colonial edifice was fortified—a reasonable precaution in the days of pirates and English attacks.

Further up Avenue de la Victoire, the **Victory Monument** commemorates French soldiers who died during the two world wars. Just before it, on the left, the **cathedral** dates from 1829. Modern stained-glass windows pour light onto the teak pulpit.

The old **town hall**, with a courtyard featuring a bronze fountain, was built in the mid-

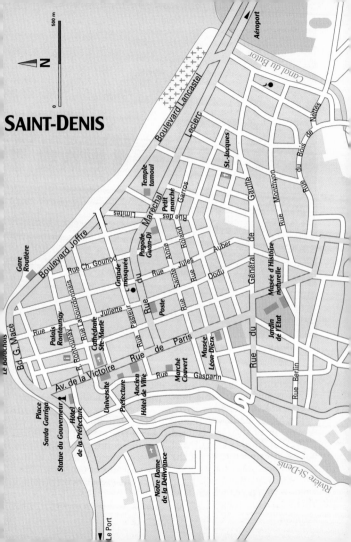

SAINT-DENIS

500 m

N

Aéroport

Canal du Butor

Boulevard Lancastel

Boulevard Leclerc

Rue du Bois de Nèfles

Rue de Monthyon

St-Jacques

Temple tamoul

Rue Garos

Petit marché

Rue Maréchal

Rue des Limites

Rue Anne

Rue Roland

Rue Sainte

Rue Jules

Rue de Gaulle

Pagode Guan-Di

Rue Ch. Gounod

Boulevard Joffre

Gare Routière

Grande mosquée

Rue Auber

Rue Dodu

Rue du Général

Musée d'Histoire naturelle

Rue Labourdonnais

Rue Ch. Gounod

Rue du

Rue Pasteur

Rue de la Poste

Jardin de l'État

Rue Rontaunay

Palais Rontaunay

Rue Juliette

Rue de Paris

Musée Léon-Dierx

Rue Berlin

Cathédrale Ste-Marie

Bd. G. Macé

Rue

Le barachois

Av. de la Victoire

Université

Préfecture

Ancien Hôtel de Ville

Marché Couvert

Rue Gasparin

Place Sarda Garriga

Statue du Gouverneur

Hôtel de la Préfecture

Notre Dame de la Délivrance

Le Port

Rivière St-Denis

With their wooden-lace trimmings, the beautiful colonial homes are today a protected species.

19th century. In the 1970s power was shifted to a big new *mairie*, in Rue Pasteur.

The rue de Paris, continuing Avenue de la Victoire, is lined with delightful old colonial houses. Designed to resist the tropical heat, they have verandas, shady gardens, and large windows to encourage air flow. There are more colonial houses to be seen in the town centre, notably in Rue Juliette-Dodu.

Continuing along Rue de Paris, you will soon reach the **Léon Dierx Museum**. Housed in the former Bishop's residence, nicely restored, it displays works of Gauguin, Vlaminck and French masters mainly of the Barbizon school. Léon Dierx was a local writer, poet and painter. Next door to the museum, the **Artothèque** is a collection of modern art displayed in a lovely Creole villa.

At the end of the street, the **Natural History Museum** was established in a 19th-century neoclassical building that once served as the law courts, set in a charming botanical garden, the **Jardin de l'Etat**. On show in the museum is an absorbing collection of Indian Ocean fauna, most amazingly a prehistoric fish, a coelacanth, thought to be extinct until this 300-kg (660-lb) whopper was hooked in 1938. Upstairs are some extinct birds, including a dodo, the emblem of Mauritius.

For insight into the multiracial character of the island, have a look at some of the religious centres in Saint-Denis. The **pagoda** in Rue Sainte-Anne, near the Petit Marché, serves the local Chinese Buddhist community. The modern Tamil **temple**, a multi-coloured Hindu establishment in Rue du Maréchal-Leclerc, is dedicated to the Lord Shiva. Twice a year the Tamil Indians walk on fire. Further up the same street, the **Grand Mosque** of Saint-Denis, one of seven mosques on the island, was built in 1970. It serves the Indian Muslims.

Saint-Denis's markets (one outside, one covered) draw visitors as much for their lively mix of inhabitants as for the choice of craftswork and appetizing fresh food. The daily **Petit Marché**, on the corner of Rue de l'Océan and Rue du Maréchal-Leclerc, sells fruit, vegetables, flowers and poultry. The **Grand Marché**, in a building enclosed in attractive iron railings at the other end of Rue du Maréchal-Leclerc, displays handicrafts, most of them made in Madagascar.

Before you leave Saint-Denis for a tour of the island, head up in the direction of the old road that passes through La Montagne to **Quatre Canons,** for a superb view over the town.

Winged Hero

A statue and a street in Saint-Denis honour Roland Garros (1888–1918), a pioneering aviator who was born here. (He is also remembered at the Roland Garros stadium in Paris, the home of the French Open tennis championships.) He was the first pilot to fly across the Mediterranean (in 1913) and is credited with making possible aerial combat by devising the synchronized machine-gun that could fire through the whirling propellor. He died towards the end of World War I, shot down at the age of 30.

Around the Island

The west coast is the warmest and the most touristic of Réunion. Go past the Pointe des Galets headland—a familiar landmark to visiting ocean liners for decades—and Le Port to reach **Saint-Paul**, the former island capital and now the second-largest town. The town hall, dating from the days of the *Compagnie des Indes*, is worth seeing, but Saint-Paul's most interesting sight by far is the old **cemetery** by the sea. This is the last resting place of the notorious French pirate La Buse, *né* Olivier Le Vasseur. He went to the gallows in 1730, daring everyone to unearth his legendary treasure of gold and diamonds. Some people are still searching for it. The French poet Leconte de Lisle is also buried here. Opposite the cemetery is a vast **grotto** where some of the earliest inhabitants of Réunion found rudimentary shelter in 1646.

A detour inland takes you through snake-like turns and up into the foothills of the Grand Bénare mountains. Creeping higher, you reach **Piton Maïdo**, at 2,200 m (7,218 ft) more than two-thirds of the way to the summit culminating at 2,896 m (9,500 ft). The name Maïdo means "burned earth", and the area is vulnerable to brush fires. If you look down over the edge into the Mafate crater's yawning "valley of death"—a jungle of almost impenetrable green—you'll find the view more thrilling than did escaping slaves who passed here 200 years ago with nowhere else to run to. (The Mafate *cirque*, or ravine or amphitheatre, is said to be named after one of the slaves, who found a rough refuge in its depths, the island's wildest terrain.) An alternative inland route through Bernica takes you to an impressive gorge and on to **Trois-Bassins**, where three waterfalls cascade down from the heights, forming pools where it is safe to bathe.

The coast road from Saint-Paul curls round the westernmost point of the island, Pointe des Aigrettes, revealing a succession of resorts that stretch all the way from beautiful Boucan-Canot to Petite Ile in the south. The beaches here of gold or black sand are edged by casuarina trees and protected by offshore reefs which create an enviable lagoon. The most developed holiday complex is at **Saint-Gilles-les-Bains**, with its array of villas, luxury hotels and restaurants. Yachtsmen, game fishermen and surfers are well served here. The best beaches are Boucan-Canot to the north and Hermitage to the south. Near Hermitage, the Jardin d'Eden (Garden of Eden) is a sensationally fragrant spot, a botanical garden specializing in spices and medicinal plants; more than 700 species are displayed and identified.

Another resort, **Saint-Leu**, was once a flourishing coffee-producing centre, as witnesses the handsome town hall, an old building of the Compagnie des Indes. The church tower provides a panoramic view along the coast.

On the outskirts of the town, la **Ferme Corail** is a nursery for sea turtles. Up to 25,000 of these creatures, reared from eggs deposited on uninhabited islets offshore, may be in residence at any one time, before being returned to the sea.

Another attraction of the Saint-Leu area, the **Stella Matutina Museum**, is devoted to the development of agriculture and industry on the island. The emphasis is on the sugar cane saga—it's still the principal crop and export earner, and covers more than half the island's arable land. Sugar mills transform the cane into a powder, then a syrup which in turn solidifies into brown sugar. In this state it's shipped to Marseilles for refining.

To the south in the direction of Saint-Pierre you can see the water spouts, **Souffleurs**—jets of spray pumping high into the air, rather like geysers, as the ocean waves surge through underwater holes in the rocks.

The far south really starts at **Saint-Pierre**, the southern "capital". The climate in this region is more humid, the sea more blue and the lifestyle more relaxed. With a population of 40,000, Saint-Pierre is at once a busy seaside resort and an important historical city. The 18th-century town hall in grand colonial style once served as a warehouse for the Compagnie des Indes Orientales, and there are still a lot of Creole houses in the centre. Visit the two pleasant markets then walk to the Hindu temple at the western end of town, one of the most re- 31 markable in the island with its statues and colourful frescoes. The town also has a big modern mosque. Across the mouth of a river lies the sleepy fishing port of **Terre Sainte**.

If you follow the coast, **Saint-Joseph**, the southernmost town, marks the halfway point of your journey. Just before it, Grand-Anse, much appreciated for its pale sand beach sheltered by basalt cliffs, will be your last chance for a bathe. But be careful: the undertow is dangerous and the coral prickly. After Saint-Joseph, you can take a side trip beside the **Langevin** river along a road that takes you through avocado and lychee plantations.

The southeast coast is the most rugged and the most beautiful of all. It begins after Pointe Langevin. From here to Sainte-Rose, the shadow of La Fournaise volcano looms over a startling landscape of jagged cliffs and deserted beaches, and scarcely a soul in sight. This is the most vivid green landscape on Réunion, much of it visibly scarred by volcanic lava from La Fournaise. In 1986 so much lava overflowed, steamed into the sea and solidified that 25 ha (62 acres) of territory was added to the municipal area of Saint-Philippe. At **Cap Méchant** on one side of town and the **Jardin volcanique** on the other, ominous black cliffs drop sheer into the waves, creating an eerie atmosphere that can almost make you shudder.

Get your wits together in **Saint-Philippe**, a peaceful little town with a small fishing harbour. Surrounded by trees of different coloured woods—white, grey, red—is a Spice and Herb Garden laid out beneath fruit trees and aromatic plants.

From Saint-Philippe it's just a stone's throw to some of the finest and biggest forests of the south. To the north of town, **Grand Brûlé** is a huge, calcinated forest. At the foot of the volcano, overlooking the sea, it has been ravaged time and time again by eruptions of the volcano. But little by little, nature is claiming its rights, and shoots of green are pushing their way through the black rock. In a similar landscape, the *Symbiose pour volcan et oiseau* is the work of the sculptor Mayo. This "Symbiosis for volcano and bird" is composed of a dozen structures carved from the lava of the 1976 eruption and surrounding a synthetic crystal placed to capture the light.

South of the village of Bois-Blanc, where lava has reshaped part of the coastline, you can see an unusual **statue** of the Virgin Mary carrying a parasol. It es-

N ←

10 miles

5

0

Pointe des Cascades

Pointe de la Table

Tremblet

Le Baril

St-Philippe

Vincendo

Langevin

Basse-Longue
Vallée

Mare
Longue

Les Lianes

La Crête

Grand Galet

St-Joseph

Piton de la
Fournaise 2631 m

Bois-Blanc

Piton
Ste-Rose

Pointe des Cascades

Ste-Rose

Plaine
des Sables

Pas de
Bellecombe
2311m

Grand
Coude

Grand
Bassin

Petite-Île

Grands-Bois

Nez-de-
Boeuf
2136m

La Plaine
des Cafres

Le Vingt-Septième

Bourg-Murat

La Plaine des
Palmistes

Beaufonds

Ste-Anne

La Confiance

Takamaka

Hell-Bourg

Forêt
de
Bébour

Bérive

Le Tampon

Les Trois
Mares

Terre
Sainte

Bois
d'Olives

Ravine
des Cabris

La Rivière

St-Pierre

Pierrefonds

Entre-Deux

Étang-Salé

St-Louis

Le Pavillon

Bras sec

Cilaos

Îlet
à Cordes

CIRQUE
DE
CILAOS

Les Makes

Les Avirons

Stella

St-Leu

Étang
St-Leu

Le Tévelave

Les Colimaçons

Trois Bassins

La Saline-
les-Hauts

La Saline
les-Bains

L'Hermitage-les-Bains

St-Gilles-les-Bains

St-Gilles-les-Hauts

Le Bernica

Petite
France

Le Bois-
de-Nèfles

Sans
Souci

Dos-d'Âne

Cap Noir

La Possession

Le Port

Pointe des
Galets

Boucan-Canot

Pointe des
Aigrettes

Savannah

St-Paul

La Montagne

St-Denis

St-François

Le Brûlé

CIRQUE
DE
MAFATE

Piton des
Neiges
3069 m

Grand
Bénard
2896 m

Piton Le
Maïdo
2203 m

Le Bélier

Îlet à
Vidot

Salazie

SALAZIE

CIRQUE
DE

Mare à Poule d'Eau

Voile de la Mariée

Abondance

Bras Canot

Rivière-
du-Mât

St-André

Cambuston

La Bretagne

Bagatelle

Ste-Suzanne

Ste-Marie

Quartier-Français

Le Colosse

Le Champ Borne

La Rivière des Roches

Bras-Panon

La Rivière du Mât

St-Benoît

RÉUNION

INDIAN
OCEAN

caped untouched when everything all around was engulfed by eruptions of La Fournaise, an event that helped to consolidate the faith of many believers. The statue was originally set up by a villager to protect the vanilla plantations. It has become a place of pilgrimage, especially on August 15 (Assumption).

Another miracle happened at Piton-Sainte-Rose, destroyed at Easter 1977 by an eruption. In the church of **Notre-Dame des Laves**, you can see photographs witnessing how the lava flow entered by the church door and stopped just in front of the altar. Just outside **Sainte-Rose**, 4 km (2 1/2 miles) away, stands a monument to Admiral Corbett, who did his duty rather too well during a sea battle against the French in 1809, the year Britain briefly also ruled the waves around Réunion. You will also see ancient cannon pointing out to see. A suspension bridge built more than a century ago straddles the Rivière de l'Est (East River). From there, the road leads to **Sainte-Anne**, whose **church** has a curious dual personality—fanciful "baroque" exterior gives way to naive frescoes inside, the work of local children.

Along this inhospitable coast, the cliffs occasionally tear apart to allow access to the ocean.

Tasty Orchid
Mexico is the birthplace of vanilla, a flavouring as tasty as it is difficult to produce. The source is a species of orchid requiring just the right altitude, climate, sun and shade, whose pod contains the flavourful beans. On La Réunion experiments with vanilla cultivation began early in the 19th century, but success depended on a method of pollination by grafting which was discovered in 1841. Vanilla is an important, labour-intensive export crop. You can see how it's done at the Vanilla Cooperative in Bras-Panon, where vanilla souvenirs are on sale.

Daring little jetties have been built for fearless sailors and fishermen to tie up their boats. The most spectacular of these creeks are at Sainte-Rose and Bourbier, near Saint-Benoît. A few fishing boats also make landings at **Anse des Cascades** (Waterfall Bay), a beautiful stopping point to view the waters tumbling over the east-coast cliffs and into the sea from the tropical hinterland.

The **windward** coast, the rainiest, starts at Sainte-Anne. The region is agricultural and has served as a magnet for workers from all points of the globe. In the 19th century tens of thousands of Tamils from southern India immigrated here. The community has preserved its customs and religion, especially at **Saint-André**. Here you can visit a museum devoted to the culture of one of the world's most fragrant flavourings, the Maison de la Vanille. You can learn more about the black and wrinkled pod at the Bourbon Vanilla Cooperative in Bras-Panon, a little further to the south.

Above Bras-Panon, in the midst of luxuriant vegetation, the Bassin de la Paix is a lovely pool of translucent water, fed by a gentle cascade.

A more turbulent sight awaits at **Takamaka,** along the Marsouins river. A narrow road winds around the sugar cane fields then plunges into the foothills. At the end of the road lies the fantastic vision of gushing waterfalls, deep gorges and rocky peaks, their summits draped in cloud. At **Sainte-Suzanne**, the so-called Niagara Falls are popular with picknickers.

The Interior
The Plaine des Cafres in the southwest and the Plaine des Palmistes in the northeast are separated by the Bellevue pass, forming a barrier over the island at 1,600 m (5,250 ft). Both plains afford access to Réunion's volatile volcano, the Piton de la Fournaise (literally, the Furnace) and both are popular with hikers.

The town of Saint-Pierre is the best departure point for the

Plaine des Cafres. A good dual-carriageway takes you as far as **Le Tampon**, where geraniums are cultivated for the perfume industry, but thereafter the road meanders unpredictably. It seems to insist on taking you everywhere except the direction you want to go. However, in the end you'll get there. The rather rugged climate of the plain has not encouraged many settlers: there's just a handful of sheep and cattle-farmers. Over on the western side, the little hamlet (here called an *îlet*) of **Grand Bassin** slumbers on, living in a different age. Only a narrow track links the valley to the outside world. **Bourg-Murat** is the meeting point of travellers from both plains; here begins the road that takes you to the volcano. Stop first for a briefing at the **Maison du Volcan** (the House of the Volcano). The tumultuous birth of the island and the volcano's inner workings are explained in audio-visual displays and documents.

En route to the volcano, you pass the Nez de Bœuf (Bull's Nose), a vantage point at over 2,000 m (6,560 ft) offering superb views down into a river gorge. Once past the forest, the scenery changes into bleak moorland dotted with basalt rock formations. Stop at the lookout point of the Belvédère to admire the Plaine des Sables. Spreading at the foot of the volcano, this is a lunar landscape of red and black rocks. The road, now just a stony track, ends at the Pas de Bellecombe, at 2,350 m (7,710 ft).

La Fournaise is almost always smoking or bubbling or shooting fire and lava into the air. Most of the lava remains in the crater area, but when a big blow happens, the flow reaches the sea along the east coast. If it quietens down, you can follow the marked tourist trail to get closer to the crater—a walk of five or six hours. You can explore various craters including the Bory, the highest at 2,631 m (8,632 ft). Pas de Bellecombe has basic accommodation in a *gîte* (refuge) for those who want to stay overnight.

The *Cirques*

Réunion's great *cirques,* inland valley basins, were created by the erosion of the Piton des Neiges, a volcano much more ancient than the Fournaise but now extinct.

From Saint-André, the road branches off among vanilla plantations and teeters along the

The Piton de la Fournaise tends to blow its top once a year, on average.

steep gorge of the Mât river to reach the **Cirque de Salazie**, the greenest of the three valleys. Everything seems to grow here, from tobacco and sugar cane to coffee beans and even apples. The slopes are alive with movement as dozens of waterfalls stream down over the rock and out of sight, momentarily swallowed up by foliage before reappearing lower down. Pause, perhaps, at the **Voile de la Mariée** (Bride's Veil) waterfall further on. The road continues to the old spa resort of **Hell-Bourg**, in a stunning mountain setting. It has preserved several attractive Creole dwellings, for instance the Folio house and garden.

From Saint-Paul or Saint-Denis, the roads to the **Cirque de Mafate** have to struggle to conquer the passes. You have to leave your vehicle behind and continue on foot to discover this valley at the end of the world. The few hundred inhabitants get their supplies delivered by helicopter.

In contrast, the **Cirque de Cilaos** seems positively lively, with a real town in the centre. Leaving from Saint-Louis, the

Weaving in and out of the forest, the trickles of water they call the Voile de la Mariée.

road passes through tobacco plantations and into a narrow valley leading to **Cilaos**, high on a rocky platform surrounded by some of the island's most formidable mountains. Cilaos is a thriving health spa resembling a French alpine resort. There are several good hikes from here, the most rewarding being the climb up **Piton des Neiges**. You can reach the peak in two days from Cilaos, staying overnight in a mountain refuge.

Dining Out

The intricacies of French cuisine are honoured, but Réunion's melting pot emphasizes creole cooking. The most typical of creole dishes is *cari*—a plate of meat (beef, young goat, chicken), tuna fish or crayfish in a tangy sauce involving garlic, onion, tomatoes, cloves, turmeric and ginger. As an accompaniment, you may have rice, peas or beans, *brèdes* (similar to spinach) and *rougails* (made of vegetables or tomato).

Another delicacy—if you can overcome any mental block—is *tangues* (hedgehog), prepared as a *cari* or stew. Cilaos lentils served with fresh salted pork give a unique flavour.

The choice of desserts is extensive, ranging from guava cream to candied papaya, 39

Cultural Notes

Creole. Probably derived from the Portuguese *crioulo*, designating a person of European parentage born in the colonies, the name Creole has varied usage in different places. In Réunion it refers to people of African ancestry. The creole language developed from the end of the 17th century, to overcome difficulties of communication between planters and slaves. The slaves themselves, from many different African countries, could not even understand one another. Creole incorporates elements of Hindi, Tamil and Chinese, as well as many African languages, together with ancient French regional expressions ; its grammar is a combination of French and African.

Beliefs. From the vast number of Hindu temples, mosques, churches and chapels, statues of the Virgin and *pti bon dié* (shrines) dotting the island, you will soon gather that the Réunionnais are very religious. Their belief in the divine and the occult are closely linked, and during the centuries, the doctrines of 17th and 18th-century catholicism have becom entangled with elements of Islam, Hinduism and African sorcery. A key figure in island life is the *charlatan*, a Malagasy witch doctor, who is able to cast spells and bewitch people. Exorcists, magnetizers and other specialists of the irrational do a roaring trade. The tombs of notorious criminals, such as the pirate La Buse, or Sitarane, who was guillotines, are almost considered as shrines, and in case of misfortune, the people pray to the spirits of their ancestors or long-dead clergymen. In emergencies, they turn to the expeditious and much revered Saint Expeditus (Expédit).

Séga. Réunion's rich musical heritage is essentially derived from African rhythms, as illustrated by the séga, similar to the calypso. Immensely popular in all the islands of the Indian Ocean, the séga dance originated in the plantations. It provided the slaves with their only entertainment, and for their descendants today, it forms a link with their ancestral roots. Accompanied by maracas and the triangle, the séga throbs to the sound of the *ravane*, a tightly stretched drum. As the minutes pass by, the rhythm accelerates, sending the dancers into a trance, then slows down into a *maloya*, representing a sign of protest, which was long prohibited.

sweet-potato cakes, fruit salads and sorbets. Bananas and pineapples grow year-round, while the seasonal fruits come in a mouthwatering array.

Although some wine is produced in the higher regions of the Cilaos valley, imported French wine and liqueurs are popular. But La Réunion's national drink is rum. The local beer is good and refreshing. La Réunion is a coffee-producing country, and a delicious variation on standard coffee, *café coulé*, spices the coffee with another local product, vanilla.

Shopping

Ash trays and figurines made from volcanic rock make good souvenirs, and you will find it hard to resist the delicate carv-

41

ings of olivewood, tamarind and ironwood. A small bottle of vetiver, ylang-ylang or geranium essence will fit easily into your luggage. The islanders are justifiably proud of their patchwork rugs, quilts and cushions. Don't miss the intricate table linen produced at the cloister of Cilaos. (The technique, taught by the local nuns, was imported from Brittany.) Artisans skilfully transform leaves into sturdy handbags, trays and hats, and in a uniquely Réunion touch, baskets are woven of vanilla pods.

Practical Information

Banks are normally open Monday to Friday 8 a.m.–4 p.m.

Climate and Clothing. The windward (east) coast is generally damp, the leeward (west) coast drier, but there are many micro-climates. Essentially there are only two seasons: the mild, dry winter (highest temperatures around 25°C/77°F on the coast), from May until November; and the summer (temperatures up to 30°C/86°F on the coast) from November until May. The most humid months are January, February and March—the cyclone season. For the cities and coastal regions, light clothing—if possible, cotton—should be sufficient. Stout walking shoes and a woollen jumper are advisable for excursions into the mountains, where it is much cooler.

Credit cards are widely accepted.

Currency. Réunion has the same currency as metropolitan France, the Euro, divided into 100 cents.

Electricity. 220 volt, 50-cycle AC.

Health precautions. Visitors arriving from infected areas must be vaccinated against yellow fever and cholera. There is no risk of malaria in Réunion.

Language. The official language is French. Among themselves the islanders speak a rich Creole.

Medical help. There are hospitals, medical centres and pharmaceutical facilities throughout the island, and no shortage of doctors. Most doctors accept holiday travel insurance certificates.

Shops. In Saint-Denis, shops are open Monday to Saturday 8.30 a.m.–noon and 2.30–6 p.m.

Time. GMT + 4.

Water. Island tap water is said to be safe to drink, but when in doubt stick to bottled mineral water, available in restaurants and bars.

SEYCHELLES

Coral and Granite

The Seychelles islands lie spattered across the Indian Ocean as though flicked there by a painter's brush. Each is a drop of green, punctured by pink granite outcrops and rimmed in white sand. The trade winds are soft through the coconut fronds, the frangipani smells sweetly at nightfall when astonishingly dramatic violet and orange sunsets pattern the sky, and at quiet moments in the day the islands' rare birds will dart out of the trees to inspect you. Everything on these unspoilt islands seems friendly, courteous and clean. The land gives coconuts, mangoes, bananas, breadfruit, pineapples, and an equally bountiful sea yields up tuna, snapper, barracuda and kingfish. Copra (coconut) and cinnamon are the main exports but the islands' tourism is the chief source of income.

The granite outcrops are unique to the Seychelles. Eons ago, India was joined to Africa. The shores receded, the ocean advanced. The Seychelles archipelago, where coral has formed around granite remains, is evidence of this ancient geological change. The main group of islands is granitic but about 60 others are coralline, low-lying and covered with dense vegetation. These include Aldabra, with the world's largest tropical lagoon.

A hundred islands and islets make up the Seychelles, yet the total land area is a mere 454 sq km (175 sq miles). The archipelago lies 1,600 km (1,000 miles) east of Mombasa, 4 degrees south of the equator. The population numbers nearly 80,830 Seychellois, of French, British, Indian, Chinese and African origin. Among themselves, most Seychellois speak Creole, a French patois. Nine out of ten live on Mahé, the largest island, 27 km (17 miles) long and 8 km (5 miles) wide, with Victoria as the capital city. Most of the hotels are on this island, but even so it's far from crowded since the coastline boasts 68 beaches and coves. There's a good international airport on Mahé and an excellent deep-water harbour. The Morne Mountains form a backdrop to the town, a region of threading streams, ferns and moss tempered by smooth boulders.

On the less inhabited islands is an abundance of rare birds and plants, giant tortoises, turtles and spectacular tropical fish. Snorkelling here is usually known as goggling, and "goggle" you will at the brilliant underwater ballets going on in the coral gardens. Most famous of all the Seychelles' rare plant species is the giant, legendary aphrodisiac *coco-de-mer* palm. This is a gentle world, where the insects are strictly non-poisonous, there are no snakes, and even the fish are unafraid of men. The most explosive sight you'll see is a flamboyant tree in full scarlet bloom, or a bougainvillaea vine pouring over a wall in a cascade of molten purple.

A Brief History

Early times	The Arabs know these islands from the 9th century on, but most shipping stays in the safer waters of the African coast.
16th–17th centuries	Vasco da Gama visits in the course of his second journey to India (1502). The islands are claimed by Portugal but not colonized, and they remain practically untouched for another 200 years.
18th century	A Frenchman, Lazare Picault, is sent to explore the Indian Ocean in 1742. He finds the main island and calls it Abondance. Two years later he returns and renames the island Mahé after Mahé de La Bourdonnais, governor of Réunion and Mauritius, who sent him on this mission. The French take official possession after the Seven Years' War in 1756 and call the archipelago "Séchelles" in honour of Moreau de Séchelles, Finance Minister to France's Louis XV.
19th century	In 1810 the British show interest in the archipelago but are forestalled by the French governor who surrenders the town and its dependencies but replaces the Union Jack by the French flag as soon as the British disappear over the horizon. The stratagem is soon discovered and the British take Mauritius, though the French governor maintains his post. British sovereignty over all the Indian Ocean islands is ratified by the Paris Treaty in 1814.
20th century–present	The Seychelles become a British Crown Colony in 1903. In June 1976 the islands gain their independence. Mancham, president of the Republic of the Seychelles, is ousted by a coup in 1977. France-Albert René sets up a single-party system. The first multi-party elections for 16 years are held in 1993, René defeating Mancham, the main opposition leader. In the 1990s, tourism overtakes fishing as the most important activity. In 2004, the long-serving president René is succeeded by James Michel.

45

Sightseeing

Mahé

This is the largest island of Seychelles and the only one with a town, **Victoria**. Even if your mind is set on the beaches, you'll want to look around this appealing settlement, founded in 1778 and capital of Seychelles since 1903. It was named Port of Victoria in honour of the British queen after her coronation.

The town centre clusters around **Freedom Square**. The Clock Tower, looking like Big Ben in miniature, was actually modelled on Little Ben, which used to stand on London's Vauxhall Bridge Road. It was erected in 1903 to commemorate the Seychelles accession to the status of colony.

Almost opposite, in front of the white-painted wooden Law Courts building, stands another relic of colonial times. On top of an old fountain, the little **statue** of Queen Victoria is a copy of the original, at 35 cm (14 in) the smallest in the world. It was set up in 1897 to celebrate the 60th anniversary of Victoria's reign, then removed to the Carnegie Library (now the National History Museum) when Independence was proclaimed in 1975. Many of the inhabitants believed the statue to represent a saint, and you may still see people crossing themselves as they pass the fountain.

From the roundabout, Independence Avenue, lined by banks and air companies, leads down to the port and ferry terminal. The **National Museum of Natural History**, guarded by a big plaster crocodile, has good exhibits devoted to marine life and the coco-de-mer. Further along the avenue, on the ground floor of Independence House, the Tourist Office offers a good choice of maps and brochures.

At the intersection with 5th June Avenue stands a statue representing the three continents of Europe, Africa and Asia, whose inhabitants originally populated the Seychelles. They are symbolized by three pairs of birds' wings. If you continue south along this avenue, you will come to another distinctive statue, a stylized bronze figure snapping a chain, erected in 1978 to commemorate the revolution of the previous year. Behind it is the Popular Stadium, inaugurated by Princess Margaret in 1972. The land of this modern area was reclaimed from the sea. Opposite is the **Old Port** and offshore lies Hodoul Island and its two powder magazines. The island was named in honour of the pirate Jean-François Hodoul who built

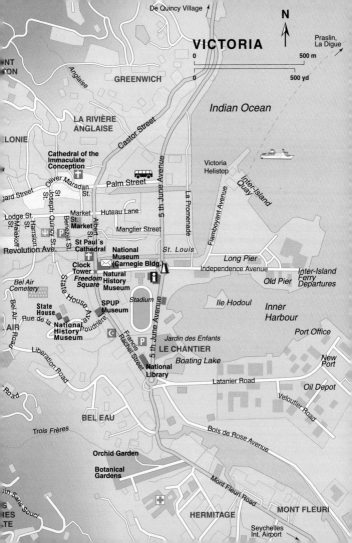

De Quincy Village

N

VICTORIA

Praslin,
La Digue

0   500 m

0   500 yd

GREENWICH

Indian Ocean

LA RIVIÈRE
ANGLAISE

Castor Street

Victoria
Helistop

Inter-Island
Quay

Cathedral of the
Immaculate
Conception

Palm Street

Oliver Maradan St.

St. Joseph St.

Quincy St.

Huteau Lane

La Promenade

5th June Avenue

Flamboyant Avenue

Market
St.
Market

Manglier Street

Lodge St.

Harison St.

Benezet St.

Albert St.

St. Louis

Revolution Ave.

St Paul's
Cathedral

National
Museum
(Carnegie Bldg.)

Long Pier

Independence Avenue

Inter-Island
Ferry
Departures

Clock
Tower
*Freedom
Square*

Natural
History
Museum

Old Pier

Bel Air
Cemetery

SPUP
Museum

Stadium

Ile Hodoul

Inner
Harbour

State
House

Bel Air Road

State House Ave.

Rue de la Poudrière

Port Office

National
History
Museum

5th June Avenue

Francis Rachel Street

Jardin des Enfants

LE CHANTIER

Liberation Road

National
Library

Boating Lake

New
Port

Latanier Road

Oil Depot

Veloutier Road

BEL EAU

Bois de Rose Avenue

Trois Frères

Orchid Garden

Botanical
Gardens

Mont Fleuri Road

MONT FLEURI

HERMITAGE

Seychelles
Int. Airport

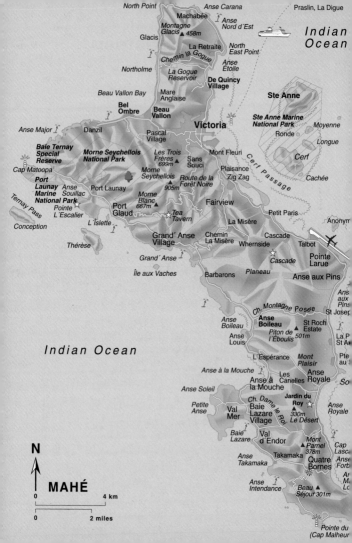

a jetty (which no longer exists) over the marshes between the island and mainland in 1800.

Going down 5th June Avenue, you come to a big modern building shared by the National Archives and the National Library, then a roundabout with a statue in the middle. From here, take Francis Rachel Street, lined by souvenir stalls, back to the clock tower. You will pass the mosque on the way.

State House Avenue winds up from the square to, where else, **State House**, the old seat of government in the middle of beautiful grounds (unfortunately closed to visitors). Just before the entrance to State House, surveyed by an armed guard, the **National History Museum** has a few old French cannon adorning the staircase. Apart from important documents relating the trials and tribulations of the islands' history, you can inspect the "stone of possession" by which the French claimed their rights to the islands in 1756. It was the custom not to plant the national flag but to lay a stone.

Facing the taxi stand and bus station, **St Paul's Cathedral**

A silver clock that never chimes: its pendulum fell overboard during unloading.

overlooks Freedom Square. It has undergone many changes since it suffered damage during a cyclone in 1862. The interior, with a single nave, is unadorned and extremely simple.

Traces of Victoria's colonial past are most obvious in the district around the market, which you'll reach by following Revolution Avenue before turning right into Benezet Street. The **Selwyn-Clarke market** is held in a modern building resembling a Chinese temple. The best and busiest time to go is Saturday morning (it closes around noon). The neighbouring district, centred on Market Street, is crammed with the tiny shops of Indian and Chinese fabric and hi-fi dealers; note the hairdressing salons, relics of a bygone era.

Cross over into Church Street to see the huge **Cathedral of the Immaculate Conception** looming over the town centre. The three-naved building was completed in 1874. The life of Mary is related in the stained-glass windows. On a hill in the park behind the cathedral, an unusual **bell-tower** with four bells chimes every hour—then again two minutes later, just in case no one heard the first time.

In the park west of the cathedral is the **House of the Swiss Capuchins**. With its arcades and balconies, many consider it the islands' loveliest building.

Take a bus or taxi for a short ride south to discover the Seychelles' fantastic flora and fauna in the **Botanical Gardens**, spreading over 6 ha (15 acres) to the foot of the mountain. There are several of the famous coco-de-mer palms here, and giant Aldabra turtles in a separate enclosure. You could also make a detour to visit the **Bel Air cemetery**, southwest of the town centre in an attractive residential district. Among the crumbling tombs is that of the notorious pirate Hodoul, much respected by the Seychellois, bearing the terse inscription "He was just." Another tomb, inscribed "Pierre-Louis Poiret", is believed by the Seychellois to be that of the lost son of Louis XVI and Marie-Antoinette.

To survey this island paradise, drive inland along Sans Souci Pass into **Morne Seychellois National Park**. Two stopping-places provide especially superb lookouts, and you can also visit a tea plantation and factory on the way. Many of the colourful houses you'll see are made up of just one room on stone or concrete foundations. In the tropical forest you'll recognise banana trees, papayas, mangoes, breadfruit and coconut palms.

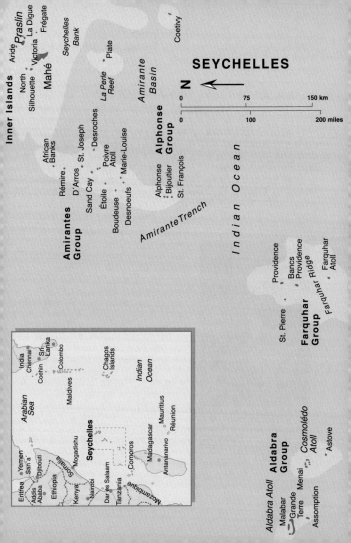

Beaches are an individual matter. **Beau Vallon**, on the north coast, is the biggest and perhaps the best. Its long, semi-circular stretch of white sand studded here and there with massive clumps of granite and fringed with palm trees is very well equipped for water sports. At noon, watch the fishermen dragging their catch onto the beach.

Near the northern tip of the island, at **Glacis**, a marquetry workshop offers carefully finished objects in native woods.

Further west, the village of **Danzil** has a big airy church containing a statue of St Roch. The saint apparently stopped the spread of a smallpox epidemic in 1884 and is consequently revered by the Seychellois. The treasure of a pirate called La Buse is supposedly hidden somewhere in the area.

Heading south of Victoria, past the airport and the village of Cascade, where you can see the remains of an old watermill, you arrive at tranquil **Anse aux Pins**, a tree-shaded bay pro-

Coco-de-mer (*Lodoicea maldivica*)
There are only two places in the world where these jumbo-sized coconuts grow in their natural state—Praslin and Curieuse islands in the Seychelles.

The palms reach a height of over 36 m (120 ft), live for 800 years and bear a curious double nut which can weigh up to 30 kg (60 lb). The female bears fruit after 25 years. The male palm carries a long catkin made up of hundreds of tiny yellow flowerlets. A Seychellois legend says that when the moon is full the male palms stalk through the jungle to embrace the females. It takes seven years for a nut to ripen.

Under the husk the fruit resembles a well-proportioned female torso from waist to thigh. When it was found washed ashore in other places it was assumed to be an aphrodisiac. The Sultan of the Maldives was so convinced that he forbade anyone else to possess one on pain of death.

You can see *coco-de-mer* palms growing in the humid semi-jungle of the Vallée de Mai on Praslin Island. There are small examples in Victoria's Botanical Gardens. No need to fear this great nut falling on your head—for some unknown reason, they always choose to drop at night.

52

tected by a stretch of coral reef. In this area, three **plantation houses** are the only ones on Mahé to have survived the passage of time. Saint-Joseph is the seat of the Creole Institute, while Saint-Roch, built in 1970, is now the centre of a lively **Craft Village** consisting of a dozen bungalows and a restaurant. A little further away, Plaine Saint-André is the oldest; it was built in 1792 by a French settler and has been converted into a museum. Just beside it is a fascinating workshop (La Marine) where exquisite models of historical ships are crafted.

The next beach along the coast, **Anse Royale**, has majestic granite formations; one of the islands' first colonies was founded here in 1772.

Ask someone for directions to the **Jardin du Roi**. It was here, on the mountain slopes, that the botanist and governor Pierre Poivre first introduced spices to the Seychelles in 1771–72. The tropical garden includes heady plantations of vanilla, cinnamon, cloves, pepper and nutmeg, all of which are sold on the spot. There are also a few animals such as Aldabra tortoises, kept in enclosures.

At the coralline **Anse Forbans** the road turns inland towards Quatre Bornes, then to **Anse Takamaka** on the west coast. This beach is unprotected by coral reef and dangerous for swimming, like its beautiful neighbour **Anse Intendance**, which you might be lucky enough to have all to yourself.

Baie Lazare was named after the 18th-century French navigator Lazare Picault, who landed here when sent to investigate the islands on behalf of Mahé de la Bourdonnais. There's a lovely view from the pretty neo-Gothic church of St Francis of Assisi.

Sheltered by palms and takamaka trees, **Anse à la Mouche** has a good beach where tuna-fishers bring in their afternoon catch. Smaller **Anse Boileau** forms a semi-circle of sun and seclusion. **Grande Anse** is particularly popular with wind surfers. Rewarding views await if you press on to **Port Glaud**, a locality surrounded by experimental farms and one of the most frequented resorts of the archipelago.

Port Launay is another popular beach with a mysterious flight of steps at its southern end, hewn in the rock leading from the shore to the cliff-top. Some believe they are a natural phenomenon, others maintain that they must have been carved by Malays 2,000 years ago. There's nothing to prove either theory. **Anse Souillac** is set 53 among cinnamon plantations; you can buy the fragrant spice in sticks or powder for cooking or pressed into tablets to perfume your clothes cupboards. **Baie Ternay** is the end of the road; you'll have to backtrack to Port Glaud to return to Victoria.

Islands around Mahé

Lying off Victoria and Mahé's east coast are six isles, enclosed within the limits of a national marine park. Sainte-Anne was the site of the first French colony in the Seychelles but now it is closed to the public. You can visit three others: Moyenne, Ronde and Cerf. There is no regular transport to the islands, but excursions are available in ordinary or glass-bottom boats. **Moyenne**, privately owned, has a restaurant in an old Creole house. **Ronde** was a women's leper colony in the 19th century; the old village chapel is now a restaurant. **Ile au Cerf** was named after the ship of Captain Murphy, an Irish sailor who landed here in 1756. It's rather jungly and also has a restaurant.

The main islands off the west coast are Thérèse (privately-owned), Conception, and the tiny Ile aux Vaches Marines.

Silhouette

To the northwest of Mahé, Silhouette, with only a few hundred inhabitants in its 16 sq km (6 sq miles), is the third-largest of the islands. It was not named for its silhouette—seen from Beau Vallon, some think it reminiscent of a woman's profile—but for the French finance minister Etienne de Silhouette, who died in disgrace in 1767.

Strange trees and plants abound in the jungly interior: the pitcher plant with its amphora-like receptacles ready to snap their lids shut on anything silly enough to crawl inside; takamakas; sandalwood and cinnamon trees.

At **Anse Lascar**, the discovery of a number of Arab graves, now swept away by the sea, suggests a possible 9th-century Arab settlement. Built like a miniature Greek temple with Doric columns and peristyle, the mausoleum of the influential Dauban family can still be seen; their colonial 19th-century mansion has been converted into a restaurant.

Praslin

Second-largest island in the Seychelles, Praslin is linked to Mahé by air and sea. With the surrounding 15 smaller islands, it forms a separate little archipelago a 15-minute flight to the north of Mahé. It is less mountainous than its neighbour, a world of creeks, coves and for-

Let's Speak Creole

Basically owing its origins to the first settlers, the Creole spoken on the Seychelles is composed of 90 per cent French, mingled with African, Malagasy, Portuguese and English expressions. Different from the Creole languages spoken on Réunion, Mauritius and in the Antilles, Seychellois was proclaimed the official language in 1981 and is taught in the schools. It was born from the need of planters and slaves to communicate with each other, and class barriers were gradually swept aside to the benefit of understanding. Lively and imaginative, its grammar compresses nouns and articles into one, and even if you pride yourself on your knowledge of French it will take you some time to extricate a meaning from words like *delo, lisyen, lapos*—de l'eau (water), le chien (the dog), la poste (post office). Some are pure poetry: a snail is *kourpas*—ne court pas (doesn't run); a bee *mous dimyel*—mouche de miel (honey fly); a chicken *kotkot*.

est with an amazing underwater life. Cars, bicycles or mopeds can be hired to explore every inch of it.

Praslin has a population of 5,000 with the main settlements at sleepy **Grande Anse** and Baie Sainte-Anne. East of Grande Anse, a road along the Nouvelle Découverte River enters **Vallée de Mai**. In this national park, light barely filters through the overhead canopy of dense green forest and the ground is strewn with granite boulders estimated to be some 650 million years old. Palms, banana and cinnamon trees, acacias, bamboo and takamakas mingle their foliage, garlanded with lianas. The regal coco-de-mer palms tower skywards, their fan-like leaves rustling in the breeze. At the top of Coco-de-Mer Grove, look for the tallest tree—it's also the oldest, having survived eight centuries. Another strange tree, the capuchin *(Northia hornei)* produces seeds resembling the hood of a capuchin monk. A vigorous insect life flourishes, bright green geckos flick across the path, and you may hear rare black parrots, but it isn't possible to see them in the dense foliage.

The road out of the valley passes a tea plantation and coconut groves to **Baie Sainte-Anne**, some of its houses still thatched with palm leaves. Ferries from Mahé and La Digue dock in this large natural harbour. There are plenty of good swimming spots in the area but the best is lovely **Anse Volbert** on the northeast coast, which is also called the Gold Coast. Around here the granite has a pink shade, due to the presence of feldspar. Beyond is **Anse Possession**, where France claimed the island in 1768 with the traditional stone laid by Marion Dufresne, then **Anse Boudin**. Last stop is one of the most beautiful beaches in all the Seychelles, **Anse Lazio**.

Islands around Praslin

Huge takamaka and casuarina trees shade the exquisite white sandy beaches of **Curieuse** island, north of Praslin. Only 3 sq km (1 sq mile) in area, the island was named after one of the ships of explorer Marion Dufresne. A few hundred giant land tortoises, an endangered species, live here. They lay their eggs on the beach in May and June. Guardians watch over the eggs and the little hatchlings until they are old enough to fend for themselves.

The granitic **Aride**, northwest of Curieuse, is one of the most unspoiled places on earth. The second-most important nature reserve in the Seychelles after 57

Aldabra, it is home to vast colonies of seabirds: sooty terns, lesser noddies, white-tailed tropical birds. This is the only place where the lemon-scented Wright's gardenia grows.

Cousin, west of Praslin, was designated an official nature reserve in 1968 in order to protect two endangered native species, the Seychelles warbler and the hawksbill turtle. Since then an estimated 250,000 birds have taken up residence on this speck of granite. There are more than 25 species altogether, as well as several species of tortoise and lizard. To visit, you have to obtain a permit from a travel agency. The number of visitors is limited, and guided tours are authorized only on certain days of the week, while swimming and picnicking are forbidden. You usually have to transfer to a canoe to land, since the coral reef makes access difficult. Cousin's small sister Cousine is also a bird sanctuary and out of bounds to visitors.

East of Praslin, **La Digue** is the fourth largest island in the archipelago, named after another of Dufresne's ships. In sweet laziness, transport is by oxcart, by bicycle or on foot—you can walk anywhere on the island within an hour. Perhaps the most romantic of the Seychelles islands, La Digue is characterized by the unruly heaps of massive granite boulders tumbling into the sea, tinged pink at dawn, grey at noon, and glowing red in the sunset.

The most renowned beach, in fact the one that stars in all those enticing tourist brochures, is **Anse Source d'Argent**, its great granite rocks among the palm trees worn by sea and wind into sensual curves. At low tide the reef is revealed. Be careful at high tide when great breakers crash onto the white sand beach. To reach this beach you have to cross the **Domaine de l'Union**, past a huge coconut grove, a plantation house, an old-fashioned naval yard, a coprah factory, an abandoned cemetery and an enclosure holding a number of giant tortoises.

There are several other inviting **beaches** with intriguing names: Anse Sévère, the best for bathing, Patates, at the northern tip, with rocks that really do look like potatoes, Gaulettes, Grosse Roche, Banane, Fourmis, and so on. In the reserve near the village, bird-watchers may spot the rare black paradise fly-catcher, once thought to be extinct.

Rocks against the ocean in unforgettable formations.

To the northeast of La Digue is a group of smaller islands, **Grande Sœur** and **Petite Sœur**, **Marianne** and **Félicité**, largely given over to agricultural plantations.

Round Island, closer to Praslin, just off Pointe Farine, was once, like its namesake near Mahé, a leper colony, but this time for men only. The hospital buildings can still be seen.

Outlying Islands

Scores of frigate birds wheel overhead as you approach **Frégate**, the easternmost of the Seychelles islands, some 60 km (37 miles) from Mahé and about the same distance from Praslin. Once the haunt of pirates, it has all the marks of a real "treasure island"; cannonballs have been found there, and three tombs embedded in the coral reef, disclosing skeletons buried with their swords.

Hilly and woody, Frégate is the garden of the Seychelles, providing the vegetables for Mahé's market. It also has a colony of giant tortoises that amble placidly through the hotel grounds, mowing the grass.

A place for dreamers, **Bird** is a coral island far to the north with limpid waters ideal for snorkelling and bathing. It has one small hotel, and thousands of birds that fear no man.

Bird's neighbour **Denis Island** is a privately owned with a luxurious bungalow resort and good snorkelling opportunities. It's particularly suitable for lovers of deep-sea fishing.

Far to the southwest of Mahé are the less-known Amirantes islands, a dozen coral isles that were governed by Great Britain and joined to the Seychelles as recently as 1976. **Desroches**, with only a handful of inhabitants, is an hour's flight from Mahé. Covered in luxuriant vegetation, it is ringed by a fine sand beach. Snorkelling areas are well marked. Divers make for the submerged Outer Rim, a wall of coral teeming with marine life. Nature-lovers will enjoy the maze of footpaths criss-crossing the island.

Surrounded by coral reefs, the **Poivre** atoll is justly famous for its magnificent beaches, lush vegetation and incomparable opportunities for scuba diving. The Indian Ocean drops more than 1,980 m (6,500 ft), creating a diver's paradise. Even beginners can take the plunge here and explore the coral reefs, which lie close to the surface.

Dining Out

Seychellois cooking has been influenced by all the races who have lived here. The French brought that irreplaceable Gallic know-how, the Africans added spices, the Chinese contributed new taste combinations, while the Indians added a liking for hot sauces.

Fresh fish on the menu is likely to include red snapper *(bourgeois)*, barracuda *(bécane)*, shark *(requin)*, trevally *(carangue)*, kingfish and tuna, the latter often served in thick, meaty steaks.

Prawns, spiny lobster and crab are fairly common. If you choose *tec-tec* soup, you'll be eating wedge clams. The Seychellois consume about 160 pounds of seafood each a year and prepare it skilfully in every conceivable way. One of their own favourites is curried octopus, very tender and cooked in coconut milk.

You may develop a taste for local offerings like pumpkin *(giraumon)*, eggplant *(aubergine)*, *patole* (a kind of cucumber) or sweet potatoes. Rice, breadfruit, noodles and manioc often take the place of potatoes. *Gros-manger* may occasionally show up—a Creole dish composed of sweet potatoes and fish anointed by a sweetish sauce. Coconut milk is often used for cooking vegetables and fish.

Fruit forms the basis of most desserts and no wonder, given the profusion of papaya, mangoes, melons, guavas, grapefruit, lychees, pineapple and jamalac (a small, glossy, rosy fruit). Bananas appear in fruit salads, flambéed in rum or sprinkled with coconut milk. Seventeen varieties of banana grow in the Seychelles, and 14 varieties of mango.

Drinks

Imported wine is available but expensive. The Seychelles local beer provides welcome refreshment, as does the locally grown tea. Citronella infusion is the Seychellois remedy for upset stomachs. *Bacca,* fermented from cane juice, or *calou,* from coconut sap, are mostly kept for festive occasions. If you meet them, beware—they're potent!

Shopping

To dress up your beach clothes you'll be presented with a multitude of bracelets and necklaces, including unusual iridescent green snail-shell jewellery. You will also see beautiful model ships and marquetry boxes in hardwoods from local forests. Favourite timbers are *calice du pape* and *bois noir*.

The weaving and basketry reach a high standard, and some of the palm-fibre hats are temptingly crazy. Batik-look prints prove attractive, as do the resort 61 clothes which range from international chic to *paréos* (wraparounds) and T-shirts with a bright Seychelles motif or signature.

Good Seychellois artists' work and handicrafts are available in a private gallery in Victoria; some specialize in attractive scenes of island life.

Practical Information

Banks. Open Monday to Friday 8.30 a.m.–1 p.m., Saturdays 8.30–11.00 a.m.

Clothes. Cotton is best. Evening wear is informal (lightweight jackets for men, dresses or skirts for women). Beach clothes are not worn in town. Leave your raincoat at home, but take an umbrella.

Credit cards. Visa and American Express cards are widely accepted (and can be used for drawing money from automatic cashpoints), while Mastercard and Diners Club are more limited. If you have another card, check with the company beforehand.

Currency. Seychellois rupee (SCR), divided into 100 cents. Coins range from 5 cents to 5 rupees; banknotes from 10 to 100 rupees. US dollars are generally also accepted, and travellers cheques are accepted in hotels, restaurants and shops. Hotel bills must be paid in foreign currency.

Driving. Traffic drives on the left. There are paved roads on Mahé, Praslin and La Digue; elsewhere the roads are sandy tracks.

Electricity. 240 V AC, 50 Hz. British-type plugs with 3 flat pins are used.

Language. The official language is Creole, a blend of French with English and African, written phonetically. English and French are widely spoken.

Shops. Open Monday to Friday 8 a.m.–5 p.m., Saturdays 8 a.m.–noon. Some shops close on weekdays noon–1 p.m.

Tipping. In addition to service charge, waiters and taxi drivers are customarily tipped 5–10 per cent.

Time difference. GMT + 4.

Telephone. Direct dialling is available for international calls and you can buy phonecards in many grocery shops. To make an overseas call, dial 0, then the country code, area code without the initial zero and local number.

Transport. There is regular bus service on Mahé and Praslin. There is no lack of bicycles for hire. Coaches are available for airport transfers and excursions and prices are reasonable. Taxis have government-controlled rates, which are quite high.

62 **Water**. Tap water is chlorinated; bottled water tastes better.

COMORO ISLANDS AND MAYOTTE

Scented Isles

The Comoros are composed of three main islands. Grande Comore *(Njazidja)* is the largest, confronting the sea with an austere basalt foreshore broken by creeks and sandy beaches. The capital, Moroni, lies on its western coast. Above the city are a few residential villas, then vanilla and ylang-ylang plantations, forest and scrub. This gradually gives way to scorched rock near the summit of mighty Karthala, the volcano which occupies the southern part of the island. The mountain's crater is 4 km (2½ miles) in diameter. From one outlet there are intermittent puffs of smoke, but the main vent is in constant rumbling activity. It last erupted in 1977.

Mohéli *(Mwali)*, the smallest island, has flourishing forests and coconut groves. At the beginning of the 20th century there was still a Queen of Mohéli, but she ceded her kingdom to France in 1901, married a Frenchman and finished her days on a Burgundy farm.

Anjouan *(Nzwani)*, known as "the Pearl of the Comoros" or "the Scented Island" is the most populous and the most scenic of the group.

Along with a score of minor islets, Mayotte *(Maoré)*, the southernmost island, forms a small archipelago apart. When the Comoro Islands voted for independence, forming the Federal Islamic Republic of the Comoros, Mayotte chose to remain French, and it is still, officially, a Territorial Collectivity of France. The island is almost encircled by a coral reef, giving rise to a beautiful lagoon with excellent opportunities for underwater exploration. Vanilla, sugar, copra and cloves are produced in modest quantities, although even more important to the economy is the fact that the French maintain a naval base there.

Part of the Comoran population is descended from *makoas*, slaves from Mozambique, and there also seems to be a Malay strain, but Arab characteristics predominate.

Many Comorans are forced to leave to find jobs in East Africa and France. Yet the islanders are not as isolated as they may seem: for generations they have been moving around the Indian Ocean, establishing links with Zanzibar, Madagascar and coastal Mozambique.

However short your stay, you'll sense that this handful of islands, with their divergent histories and landscapes and gentle, dignified people, merits quiet, detailed exploration.

COMOROS

Grande Comore (Njazidja)

Bangoi-Kouni
Ndroudé
Mitsamihuli
Hantsindzi
Isandreni
Lac salé
Trou du Prophète
Bouni
Mbeni
Touaha
Ntsaweni
Massif de la 1084m
Touaha 860m
Grille
Maoueni
Hahaya
Itsikudi
Nvarinambwani
Voidjou
Bahani
Kwamboni
Nioumadzaha
Chimoni
Lac Hantsongoma 1100m
Kartala 2361m
Tsangadjou
Ntsudjini
Itsandra
Tsidjé
Mvouni
Pidjani
Bandamadji
Itsoudzou
Singani
Foumbouni
Moroni
Ikoni
Bobini
Kourani
Malé
Mvouni
M Bachilé
Bangoua
Mindralou
Ouroveni
Chimadjou
Chindini
Nyumadzaha
Salimani
Mdé
Moroni
✈

0   5 miles

Mohéli (Mwali)

Houani
Mirangoni
Djouayesi
Fomboni
✈
Sambia
Itsamia
Mzé Koukoulé 790m
Nyoumashoua
Ouénéfou
Méa
Chandzi
Dzaha
Marine Reserve

0   5 miles

Anjouan (Nzwani)

Ouani
Moutsamoudou
✈
Jimilimé
Hajoho
Ongoni
Bambao
Gégé
Djadjana 990m
Dindi
Trindrini
Chironkamba
Ajaho
Domoni
Sima
Bimbini
Foumbani
Marahare
Vassi
Vouani
Pomoni
Ouzini
M Rémani
Vandza
Papani
M Ramani
Bandamagi
Chaouéni
Chironi
Île de la Selle

0   5 miles

Mayotte (Maoré) (France)

Bandraboua
Baie de Boa
Trévani
Longoni
✈
Mamoudzou
Labattoir
Passamainti
Pamandzi
✈
Petite Terre
Mtsamboro
Bandrélé
Acoua
Dzani Bolé 472m
Mtsahara
Chiconi
Tsingoni
Bénara 660m
Ngouja
Dapani
Mtsamoudou
Mbouini
Dzaoudzi
Chissioli
Mtzamboro
Chiconi
Sada
Boueni
Chirongui
Choungui 594m
Kani-Kéli
Grande Terre
Dembeni
Mtsangachehi

0   5 miles

INDIAN OCEAN

MOZAMBIQUE CHANNEL

72 miles
115 km

75 km

53 miles
85 km

71 miles

(inset map)

TANZANIA

MOZAMBIQUE

Aldabra Is.
Assomption
Cosmoledo Is.
Astove
Providence
I. Du Cerf
Farquhar
Glorieuses
Nosy Be
Antsiranana

Comoro Islands

Grande Comore (Njazidja)
Mohéli (Mwali)
Anjouan (Nzwani)
Mayotte (Maoré)

N ←

A Brief History

Early times	An old legend relates that "the prophet Solomon ben David" (King Solomon of Biblical history) visits the Comoro Islands around 965 BC followed by Arabs from the Red Sea coast, their wives, children, servants and slaves.
16th century AD	The Shirazi, whose ancestors left Persia because of religious persecution, arrive. Africans follow and a chieftain system is established. By the time the Portuguese land, the Muslim religion is established. Sultanates gradually replace government by village chiefs.
17th–18th centuries	British, French and Dutch ships visit peacefully on their way to the Indies. Anjouan is their favourite island because it offers a good harbour and fresh water.
19th century	The Malagasy take control of Mayotte in 1822, and in 1830 Mahéli is conquered by Hova Ramanetako of Madagascar.

Mayotte is annexed by the French in 1841. The British, anxious to keep up with French expansion, install a Consul on Anjouan in 1849. All goes well until William Sunley is appointed and causes a scandal by owning a plantation with 600 slaves. The opening of the Suez Canal in 1869 diminishes British interest, and in 1886, Mohéli, Anjouan and Grande Comore become a French Protectorate. |
| 20th century– present | The Comoro Islands are made a French colony in 1912 and are given the status of a French Overseas Territory from 1958 to 1975, when they vote for independence. On Mayotte, the population chooses to remain French. After several coups, elections are held in 2001 and a new constitution grants greater autonomy and their own presidents to Grande Comore, Anjouan and Mohéli. These become the Union of Comoros with overall leadership assumed by Colonel Azaly Assoumani, whose jurisdiction is limited to security and finance. Ahmed Abdallah Sambi is elected President in May 2006. |

Sightseeing

Grande Comore

All of the Comoros are volcanic islands, but the youngest of them geologically, Grande Co-more, is still bubbling away. Within the depths of **Kartala Volcano**'s crater, awesome natural forces continue to rumble and fume. The rim is 2,361 m (7,746 ft) high, so this excursion is definitely not for the casual hiker.

On the north side of the island is another volcanic phenomenon, **Lac Salé**, a sea-water lake caught in a deep crater. In this case, the sight is more tranquil than menacing.

The capital of Grande Comore, and of the republic, the city of **Moroni** sprawls from the harbour into the medina. In the middle of the old town, the Mosquée du Vendredi is the religious heart of the Comoro Islands, and the **old market** couldn't be more colourful.

Near the post office, a small **museum** recounts local history and provides information on the Kartala volcano.

The best beaches are in the north of the island, in particular at **Galawa**, between Mitsamiouli and Mbeni, which boasts sparkling white sand, coconut palms and fascinating underwater life. Along the same coast, the **Trou du Prophète** is a cove where, according to legend, Mahomet found refuge.

Anjouan

Moutsamoudou, the port and capital of Anjouan island, stretches along the waterfront and rises up the slopes of Mount Hombo. Tradition has it that centuries ago, a shepherd called Moussa Moudou (Moses the Black), pastured his flock here and watered it at the little river. He prospered and left many descendants, and the town is named after him.

Get the local children to lead you into the rabbit-warren of streets backing the **port**. Here are Swahili-Shirazi style 17th-century houses with carved doors and lintels lining dim, narrow streets. As you walk by, the women whip their *chiromani* across their faces, leaving only a narrow eye-slit. Here on Anjouan this length of cotton, modestly draped around body and head, is usually brilliant scarlet and white, a tribute to the colours of the former Sultan's flag. The island has a proud Arab aristocracy. The girls won't want to uncover their 67 faces, but they'll agree to being photographed in groups, smiling shyly from behind their vivid robes.

The widest street leading inland encircles the old town and leads to a small market. If you keep to the left and climb a short distance into the hills, you'll come to Mutsamudu's **citadel**, built in the 18th century by Abdallah I with British help. It provides a good view over the city rooftops to the bay.

Domoni is the island's second most important settlement, situated on the east coast. It can be reached via **Bambao**, the perfume village, where ylang-ylang, jasmine, patchouli and orange flowers are distilled for the scent industry.

Domoni itself is the old capital of the sultans, with a 12th-century mosque. At the entrance to one of the houses you will be shown an elaborately carved medieval door, set in place after consultation with a *thaleb* (learned man) using astrology to choose the exact direction it should face and the propitious moment for hanging it. Such doors are never moved from their original position.

Mohéli

With its unspoiled, pastoral way of life, Mohéli is perfect for hiking. In the southern region,

Nyumashuma and neighbouring islets form a marine reserve, where you can see giant turtles.

Mayotte

Two islands and around twenty islets nestling in the heart of world's biggest closed lagoon compose this tiny archipelago.

Pamandzi airport is located on the island of **Petite Terre**, which is also a military base where several detachments of the army and Foreign Legion are stationed.

Mayotte is a volcanic archipelago with several craters. One of them, in the north of Petite Terre, encloses **Dziani Lake**, fringed by coconut palms. The Mahorais consider it sacred, and its green sulphurous water is reputed for healing skin diseases. The lake is easy to reach on foot. You can follow a hiking trail all round the crater, from where you'll get good views of Grande Terre, Mayotte's other main island, and over Moya beach below the volcano, where turtles lay their eggs.

Also visible from the summit is **Dzaoudzi**, a small settlement clustered on a rock. It is linked to Pamandzi by a causeway familiarly known as the *boulevard des crabes* (Crab Boulevard). Dzaoudzi was the capital of the Comoro Islands until 1962, but it is now reduced to a military and administrative centre. The Mayotte Museum is under construction; until it opens, there is little to do in Dzaoudzi but stroll around the gardens of the old Prefecture building. You can catch the boat that shuttles back and forth several times a day between Petite Terre and Grande Terre, only 3 km (under 2 miles) away.

The principal port on **Grande Terre** is **Mamoudzou**. With 40,000 inhabitants, most of them Europeans, it is Mayotte's main town, and the new administrative and trading centre of the archipelago. Apart from the **market** and the **tomb** of Sultan Adriansouli, the last ruler of Mayotte who sold the island to the French in 1841, there's little of interest in the town.

Set out to discover the hilly landscape of this fragrant, verdant island. Following the coast road you will travel through tiny villages of painted huts sweltering under the sun. You can't fail to notice the houses called *bangas,* gaily decorated with drawings and slogans. These are built by and for adolescent boys with the aim of learning how to live independently, away from their families, and to prepare them for manhood. Once married, they abandon these "bachelor pads" and go to live with their wife and her family.

From one end of the island to the other, the road plays hide-and-seek with the sea, alternately passing sandy beaches and rocky shores. The interior is shrouded in thick forest carpeting the slopes of ancient volcanoes.

The southern part of Grande Terre is the most scenic—wild, green and scored with valleys. You can climb **Mt Choungi**, 594 m (1,950 ft), for a remarkable view over the whole archipelago. Cool off with a bathe with the turtles at **Ngouja** beach—a stretch of white sand lining a little cove, edged by coconut palms, baobabs and casuarinas. You can go fishing or snorkelling, or hire a boat to discover other quiet beaches, such as Longoni, at the northern end of the island, and the Mkadijou peninsula.

At high tide, the **Soulou waterfall**, on the west coast, tumbles directly into the sea. It is well worth making a trip to this spot; a long trail winds down to a black-sand beach in an inlet where sometimes turtles come to play.

Dining Out

Restaurants offer international food with a French and local slant. There is plenty of fish and seafood even though fishing 69 methods need modernizing to supply local demand. Coconut and spicy sauces add flavour. Chicken with coconut milk is a favourite dish.

Rice is the usual accompaniment but you'll also be offered cassava and plantain, a type of large banana steamed or baked as a vegetable. Manioc leaves are the local equivalent of spinach. Couscous is served with a sauce that may be made with vegetables, fish or meat, or a combination. Snacks include salty little meat and spice cakes, but it's wise to approach street snacks with caution.

There's plenty of tropical fruit: fresh pineapples, mangoes, papaya and bananas.

Shopping

In Anjouan you will be offered shells and *chiromani*. Phials of perfume oil are sold in Bambao, the scent village. Grande Comore specializes in baskets and pottery. Takamaka wood is carved into furniture and model boats. There is some beautiful embroidery, skullcaps and slippers in particular. Also found are dolls in national costume, as well as spices.

Practical Information

Banks. Open Monday to Thursday 7.30 a.m.–1 p.m., Fridays 7.30–11 a.m.

Climate. December to March temperatures are very high and there is heavy rain at times. August and September are good diving months; November and December are recommended for deep-sea fishing.

Clothing. Light, informal, modest to conform with Islamic traditions.

Credit cards are accepted only in large hotels.

Currency. The Comoros franc (CFr or KMF, tied to the Euro, which is also accepted. The most commonly used coins are 25, 50 and 100 Cfr, banknotes from 500 to 10,000 Cfr. In Mayotte, the currency is the Euro, as in France.

Electric current. 220 volts, 2-pin plugs.

Health. Malaria precautions are necessary; ask your doctor for advise. Yellow fever and cholera injections are required if coming from an infected area. Medical facilities are limited, so bring any supplies you feel you may need.

Language. The official languages are Arabic and French. Among themselves the inhabitants speak a dialect derived from Swahili.

Time. GMT + 3.

MADAGASCAR

Chameleon Island

The old Malagasy proverb, "Destiny is like a chameleon clinging to a branch; the slightest sound and it changes colour…", could fittingly be applied to the strong hues of this island in the Indian Ocean, lying some 400 km (250 miles) off the southeast coast of Africa. Madagascar's countryside looks different behind every hill; the people, the animals and the vegetation change round every bend in the road. Beyond each bay and each headland the Indian Ocean perpetually renews the character of the beaches, the isles, the perfumes and the climate.

Is Madagascar African? Certainly no more so than its neighbour islands: Mauritius, soft, feminine, voluptuous; and Réunion, with its grandiose, tormented landscapes. Geographically, of course, this huge island forms part of the Dark Continent, but it was populated more than fifteen centuries ago by Indonesian settlers, followed by others from East Africa. The Malagasy bear a much closer resemblance to the Torajas of the Celebes, the Bataks of Sumatra or the Dayaks of Borneo than to the Kikuyu of neighbouring Kenya. The magnificent terraced paddy-fields have the same serenity as those of Java, and on the coast, the slender outrigger canoes of the fishermen were surely inspired by the *bugis* sea gypsies, those infamous pirates who still haunt the seas and archipelagos of the Philippines, Indonesia and Malaysia. Like their distant cousins from the East, Madagascans mark their major festivals by the sacrifice of numerous zebus, the humped oxen whose tender and delicate flesh gives even the Aberdeen Angus enthusiast food for thought.

All this means that the ethnic groups and cultures of Madagascar are only vaguely similar to those of the nearby African continent, where national borders are a legacy of colonialism and countries are divided by a plethora of languages. Here, on the fourth largest island of the planet after Greenland, New Guinea and Borneo, which covers an area equal to that of the countries of France and Belgium combined, one single language is spoken the length and breadth of the land. Although there are several dialects, the national tongue indisputably stems from the great family of Malayo-Polynesian languages, which includes Malay, Indonesian and Maori.

Since the rejection of Communism in 1993, Madagascar is

once again timidly opening its doors to investors, taking advantage of its natural riches and inviting tourists to enjoy its sumptuous landscapes, the gentleness and beauty of its people and the astonishing variety of its exceptional flora and fauna. Every week, a few hundred privileged visitors discover this perfumed isle. All intercontinental flights land at Antananarivo (Tananarive), the capital city "of a thousand warriors", home to 10 per cent of the 18.5 million Malagasy.

On the island, there are thousands of unique plants. Despite irrational destruction of the forests, ravaged by burning out clearings for crops or cattle, 10 per cent of the island surface is still forested and home to more than 50 kinds of lemur. In these areas, it is not unusual to find a hundred rare species of trees growing on as many square metres of land. Six varieties of baobab flourish here (the African continent only has one kind), and among the thousand species of orchid, one in particular deserves special mention: vanilla. Madagascar exports two-thirds of the world's production.

A Brief History

500 BC–300 AD	The island is thought to be uninhabited, but possibly is occupied by indigenous peoples. Arrival of first settlers from Indonesia and later from the African continent.
8th–9th centuries	Appearance of the earliest Arab trading posts around the coast.
10th–15th centuries	New waves of immigration from Malaysia and Indonesia, the legendary Vazimba civilization driven back into the forest and establishment of a true Madagascan people on the high plateau; slow destruction of the virgin forest by burning; foundation of the Merina dynasty; increase in number of Arab and Muslim trading posts.
16th century	Arrival in 1500 of the Portuguese Diego Diaz, the first European explorer; later, in 1527, arrival of French sailors from Dieppe. Reign of Rafohy and Rangita, then Andriamanelo and his son Ralambo, who names his people the Merina and creates the kingdom of Imerin' Ambaniandro.
17th century	The Portuguese, the Dutch and principally the French try to colonize Madagascar. A succession of Malagasy king-

doms follow while the French become established at Fort Dauphin in 1642. Half of the colonists are massacred in 1674, and France, which had annexed the island, withdraws. Thereafter, the coast provides refuge for pirates.

18th–19th centuries

Many clashes between various Malagasy clans and kingdoms. On assuming the throne in 1787, King Andrianampoinimerina re-establishes control, unites a good part of the island and leaves a sizeable kingdom to his son Radama in 1810. This young king, with the support of the English, introduces Christianity, a written language and schools. In 1883, France establishes a fragile protectorate. After a period of anarchy, the French seize Tananarive in 1895 and establish a second protectorate. In 1896, after an uprising and a breaking of the protectorate treaty, Queen Ranavalona III is deposed and the monarchy abolished. France decrees the colonization of Madagascar, deports the queen to Reunion in 1897 and then exiles her to Algiers in 1899.

20th century– present

The "pacification" of Madagascar continues until 1917 and encourages the rise of Malagasy nationalism. Revolution breaks out on March 27, 1947 and is only put down on December 4, 1948. The Republic is proclaimed on October 14, 1958 and Madagascar finally achieves independence on June 26, 1960. Tsiranana, the first president, is deposed by the army in 1972 and three years later Didier Ratsiraka is called to power. He turns to socialist principles. His little red book and his nationalizations isolate Madagascar from the western nations. The island suffers a serious economic crisis. In 1991, the people revolt and demand the departure of Ratsiraka. Two years later, President Albert Zafy is elected by a large majority but Ratsiraka is recalled in 1997. In the election of 2001 he is narrowly defeated by Marc Ravalomanana, officially declared the winner by the High Constitutional Court in April 2002.

Sightseeing

Madagascar is endlessly seductive. Nowhere else in Africa are the colours so vivid, the people so hospitable, the smiles so dazzling, the women so graceful, the food so delicious—and the abject poverty so well concealed.

Antananarivo
The lively streets of Tananarive, or "Tana", built on twelve hills,

MADAGASCAR

TANJONA BOBAOMBY
(Cap d' Ambre)

Ramena
Antsiranana
(Diego-Suarez)

Ambohitra

Nosy Be

Andoany
(Hell Ville)

Ambilobe

Ambanja

Ambohitra

Ihrana
(Vohémar)

Bealanana

Sambava

Antsohihy

Andapa

Antalaha

Antonibe

Antsakabary
Befandriana Ava.

Ambohitra-
lanana

Mahajanga

Boriziny

Maroantsetra

TANJONA VILANANDRO
(Cap Saint-André)

Mitsinjo

Marovoay

Mandritsara

Soalala

Mampikony

Marotandrano

TANJONA MASOALA

Sitampiky

Miarinarivo

Mananara Ava.

Besalampy

Maevatanana

Andilamena

Soanierana-
Ivongo

Nosy Boraha
(Sainte-Marie)

Mora-
fenobe

Mahabe

Kandreho

Ampara-
faravola

Fenoarivo

Vavatenina

Mahavelona
(Foulpointe)

Maintirano

Ambato-
mainty

Ambaton-
drazaka

Toamasina
(Tamatave)

Antsalova

Ankazobe

Anjozorobe

Anda-
sibe

Ampasimanolotra

Tsiroano-
mandidy

Ambohi-
dratrimo

ANTANANARIVO

Moramanga

Miandrivazo

Lac Itasy

Mantasoa

Vatomandry

Belo Tsiribihina

Faratsiho

Anosibe
An'ala

Betafo

Antanifotsy

Morondava

Antsirabe

Marolambo

Mahabo

Fandriana

Mandabe

Mandro-
narivo

Ambositra

Nosy Varika

Ambohi-
mahasoa

Manja

Ikalama-
vony

Vohilava

Fianarantsoa

Ifanadiana

Mananjary

INDIAN OCEAN

TANJONA ANKABOA
(Cap Saint-Vincent)

Beroroha

Ambalavao

Namorona

Ankazoabo

Ihosy

Ikongo

Manakara

Ifaty

Sakaraha

Vondrozo

Farafangana

Toliara
(Tuléar)

Betroka

Vangaindrano

Betioky

Ianakafy

Midongy
Atm.

Benenitra

Mahabo

Befotaka

Bekily

Ampanihy

Ste-Luce

Beloha

Amboasary

Taolanaro
(Fort Dauphin)

Tsiombe

Ambovombe

N

TANJONA VOHIMENA
(Cap Sainte-Marie)

0   50   100 miles

MOZAMBIQUE CHANNEL

Mahafaly

spill down towards Lake Anosy and the towering Hilton Hotel on its shore. The town's charm is easier to appreciate once you have toured the island and taken the time to adapt to the nonchalant rhythm of Madagascan life. Despite a good 1.5 million inhabitants, the town is unmistakably rural, at once picturesque and anachronistic, its suburbs soon giving way to paddy-fields and farmland.

The craftsmen of the lower town and the famous **"zoma"** (Friday) **market** spreading over several streets of the centre are Antananarivo's liveliest attraction. The farmers come in from the surrounding countryside every day to sell fruit, vegetables, spices, animals and a host of other produce.

Perched on a high hill dominating the town, the labyrinthine Queen's Palace, known as the **Rova**, was destroyed in a devastating criminal fire in 1995. Some of its treasures, such as the throne and crown, were retrieved and are displayed in the Andraviavata Palace while the Rova is slowly being rebuilt, with the aid of UNESCO.

Merina Country and the Highlands

The countryside around "Tana" and its sacred hills deserve a close look. Here you are in the heart of Merina country. At **Ambohidratrimo**, in front of three adjoining wooden houses containing royal tombs, two breasts sculpted on a standing stone ensure fertility to barren women who bring offerings and guarantee the birth of a male child to those who are pregnant.

At **Ambohimanga**, residence of Andrianampoinimerina and sacred town of the Merina monarchy, the Malagasy state came into being. The air of mystery surrounding this "forbidden city" brings to mind the long pages of history which were written in this holy place, protected by seven doors including that of Ambatomitsangana,

A Curious Carnivore
Madagascan flora includes a strange carnivorous plant, the *nepenthes*—but rest assured, you are not in danger of being devoured whole. Its long twisted stem ends in a cone-shaped vase containing a delicately perfumed liquid. The lid closes when some unfortunate insect, attracted by this magic potion, ventures within. At the bottom of this deadly pocket, flies, mosquitoes, butterflies and dragonflies are swallowed by the floral digestive system and dissolved in the sap. Even as digestion takes place, the lid re-opens to trap new victims.

which is still topped by a curious red lookout post. An enormous stone disc, 4.5 m (15 ft) in diameter and 30 cm (1 ft) thick, designed to block the doorway, is still in place.

Despite the history-steeped atmosphere of the highlands, nature does not take second place. Beauty spots include the shores of Lake Mantasoa, a favourite outing for the people of Antananarivo; the volcanoes which encircle Lake Itasy and the Lilha Falls that cascade into it; the thermal baths in the spa town of Antsirabe; and the rain- forest of Perinet crammed with rare trees and reached from **Andasibe** on the Toamasina road. If you get up early, you may see an *indri*, the biggest of the lemurs, or other tropical primates.

The Southwest

The biggest and best baobabs can be admired at Morondava on the west coast. Madagascar has six species, whereas the African continent can boast only one. There are also some splendid specimens of these "giant bonsai" to be seen near

An avenue of venerable baobabs some 25 km (15 miles) from Morondava.

77

Berenty, Betioky and Tulear. The graceful *ravinala*, or traveller's tree, whose trunk contains a valuable reserve of drinking water, grows in every part of the island, its branches spreading like a huge fan. But Madagascar owes most of its fragrance to coffee, cloves and especially vanilla, which is just one of the thousand varieties of orchid flowering here.

At **Morondava**, permeated by souvenirs of the ancient kingdom of Menabe, the sun shines for 300 days each year, a fact that should tempt you to enjoy its bustling fishing port or the solitude of its beaches. Near Morondava, you'll find some of the most interesting funerary monuments of the island at Antalitoko and Mangily.

The sun also beats down on **Tulear** (or Toliara), reached by a difficult but spectacular road journey. This route takes you by way of **Isalo National Park**, where you see the "monkey canyon," home to numerous lemurs, the "swimming pool" and a cave thought to have sheltered 16th-century shipwrecked Portugese sailors.

Tulear is sheltered by flame trees and tamarinds. Visitors are charmed by its port, cooled by sea breezes and animated by a shell market. The **Musée des arts et traditions populaires du Sud malgache** displays examples of the Mahafaly tombs and funerary art, the most spectacular in Madagascar.

About an hour away by car, along a track dotted with pic-

The Living and the Dead

The worship of the dead, often preceded by a sumptuous burial, is invested with very great importance in Madagascar. Each region has its specific rites. Families take care of their own dead, who are exhumed every year if the family can afford it. The *lamba*, or silk shroud in which the corpse is wrapped, is changed and the skeleton cleaned before the whole lot is put back in the tomb. The exhumation provides a pretext for great celebrations. These practices take place in perfect harmony with the doctrines of the Catholic church, which, after all, also teaches the resurrection.

Near Fort Dauphin, in Mahafaly country around Tulear, tombs often resemble small castles, their walls decorated with geometric or naive paintings. On these strange structures, covered with large stones strewn with the skulls of zebus sacrificed during the funeral ceremony, are erected *alaoa*, or totems carved with human and animal forms and objects recalling the life of the deceased.

Tombs decorated with zebu horns or carved statuettes are to be found all over the south.

turesque fishing villages, the beautiful sandy beaches of **Ifaty** offer the possibility of a quiet and relaxing seaside break in holiday bungalows clustering around a turquoise lagoon. A highly recommended excursion is by canoe to the Vezo village of **Anakao**, opposite the isle of Nosy Be.

Fort Dauphin and the South

Beyond the Onilahy river and the town of Betioky, the **Bezaha Reserve** is perfect for lovers of unusual painting and sculpture.

The royal tombs of the Mahafaly and the Antandroy ("thorn people") dot this wild land, accessible only in a four-wheel drive vehicle, and populated by people and animals scarcely touched by modern ways.

A bumpy track links Tulear to Taolanaro (Fort-Dauphin). Three hours from this oasis, the **Berenty Reserve**, one of the wildest and most interesting sites of Madagascar, offers the best possible opportunity to see the island's endemic plants and endearing lemurs performing their strange, leaping ballet. 79

You can also visit, or stay in, the **Nahampoana reserve**, 7 km (4 miles) from town.

Taolanaro/Fort-Dauphin is built on a magnificent site close to the mountains, sandwiched between the sea and the desert. It is near this pleasant resort at the gates of the jungle that you can see those strangest of carnivorous plants, the *nepenthes,* in their natural habitat.

Fort-Dauphin is a wonderful centre for excursions. It lies 53 km (33 miles) from **Sainte-Luce**, a village nestling in the most exotic scenery of the Madagascan coastline. From an explosion of tropical vegetation, myriad headlands and rocky islets arise, protecting a string of unspoilt beaches. There's no hotel here, just a nature reserve known only to local guides and drivers. Sit on the white sands, eat fresh crayfish and mangoes, and enjoy the astonishing and delightful experience of an idyllic spot where as yet no holiday village has been established.

The East Coast

On the east coast, they say the year has two seasons: the rainy season and the wet season. But the sun shines frequently between showers. Here you'll find **Toamasina** (Tamatave), the largest port of Madagascar, with an attractive floating market just as you enter the town on the road from the airport.

To learn more about Madagascar's flora and fauna and see some of the species up close, take a trip to the 282-ha zoological park of **Ivoloina**, 12 km (7 miles) from Toamasina. Several kinds of lemur roam through the grounds and there are even more in the zoo, as well as radiated tortoise, tree boas, tomato frogs, tenrecs and chameleons.

If you like beach holidays and don't mind a bit of rain, then **Mahavelona** (Foulpointe), 60 km (37 miles) north of Toamasina is the place for you. Or try the trip from Tamatave to **Ankany Ny Nofy** in the south. You go by train and return by boat along the Pangalanes Canal.

Nosy Boraha (Sainte-Marie), the island of women, no longer welcomes hopeful pirates, but the roses and wild orchids still bloom where many love stories were once played out. The endless beaches, rainbow coral and luxuriant vegetation bathed in the perfume of clove trees make this a tropical paradise where even treasure seekers don't always return empty-handed. Together with its small islets, Nosy Boraha forms an archipelago. Sainte-Marie can be explored by mountain bike. Enjoy the countryside of the north, south and east and visit the church and pirate cemetery of the "capital" **Ambotifotatra**, home of 2,000 thousand friendly inhabitants.

The North

With the finest natural harbour of Madagascar, the bay of **Antsiranana** (Diego Suarez) is often compared to that of Rio de Janeiro because of its sugar-loaf granite cone. Only 20 km (12 miles) away is the magnificent bathing beach of **Ramena** but beyond this point the comparison fades.

Named after two Portuguese explorers who first set foot on Madagascar—Diego Diaz and Ferdinand Suarez—the town of Diego Suarez is a centre from which you can make some interesting excursions. To the north, there is the wild countryside of **Cap d'Ambre**, not easy to reach but worth a visit. Make a detour on the way to see the fortified rock of Windsor Castle and the Baie des Courriers. To the south, by way of the village of Ambohitra, once known as Joffreville, is the road leading to

The Fascinating Lemur

Madagascar is home to 90 per cent of the known species of lemur worldwide. The absence of large predators has helped these attractive little animals to survive. Of the 54 species observed on the island, 32 are native. The lemurs found near Fort Dauphin in the Berenty Reserve are particularly affectionate. In the middle of this protected forest, a giant botanical garden planted with the rarest of species, a museum of Malagasy traditions has been established. It is not uncommon to be awakened at dawn by a *maki*, a somewhat bold lemur with a long black-and-white ringed tail often held in the form of a lyre, who will even come to your door to beg for his early-morning banana.

81

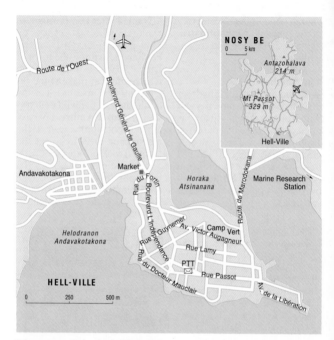

NOSY BE

0   5 km

Antazohalava
214 m

Mt Passot
329 m

Hell-Ville

Route de l'Ouest

Boulevard Général de Gaulle

Market

Andavakotakona

Rue du Fortin

Boulevard l'Indépendance

Horaka Atsinanana

Route de Marodokana

Marine Research Station

Rue Guynemer

Helodranon Andavakotakona

Camp Vert

Av. Victor Augagneur

Rue Lamy

Rue du Docteur Mauclair

PTT

Rue Passot

Av. de la Libération

HELL-VILLE

0   250   500 m

Montagne d'Ambre National Park with its waterfalls, crater lakes and lemurs, and to the crocodile-infested waters of the legendary sacred lake of **Antanavo**.

In the **Ankarana** range, thick beds of limestone have weathered into weird-shaped razor-sharp points and pinnacles known as "tsingy", forming an unearthly landscape. To the east, explore the Vanilla Coast and **Vohémar** with its picturesque Green Lake, a region which is home to the Onjoatsy people, descendants of Arab traders, and where many tombs have been discovered. The same excursion takes you to **Sambava** and the Andamoty lake, and to **Andapa**, amid paddy-fields, vanilla and coffee plantations at the threshold of the rainy **Marojezy Reserve**, wet and wild but grandiose.

Nosy Be

To the northwest, this island has everything for the water-sports enthusiast. On arrival, visitors are garlanded with flowers by charming local girls. Bordered by coconut palms, the beaches of this Madagascan Tahiti now boast good hotels where you can rest in comfort after long journeys on the rough island roads. Ylang-ylang, cultivated for the perfume industry, drowns the island in a heady fragrance. Coffee, sugar cane and spices are also grown here, and mangroves are to be found along the coast.

The French Admiral Hell, once governor of Réunion, gave his name to the main town of Nosy Be. **Hell-Ville**, a busy town of 10,000 inhabitants, has, despite its name, a certain charm and its colourful market displays all the island's fruits and spices.

Daily **excursions** are organized to the principal attractions of Nosy Be. These are the fishing village of Ambatoloaka, the western hills dominated by Mount Passot, 329 m (1,080 ft) and its curious lakes formed in volcanic craters, Djamandjary and its sugar-cane distilleries, the luxuriant vegetation of the east and the golden beaches of Andilana, Befotaka and Amporana in the north.

Ancestors in the Lake

The sacred lake of Antanavo at the northern tip of Madagascar, brimming with big crocodiles, is haunted by a singular legend.

It seems that long ago, on the site of the present-day lake, there was a village with a reputation of unfriendliness toward strangers. One day the sorcerer of another tribe turned up half-dead of thirst, but instead of assisting him the villagers tried to chase him away. For their antipathetic ways, the sorcerer put a curse on them, decreeing that they would be engulfed by the waters of a lake and inhabit its depths ever after as crocodiles.

The people today living around the lake consider the crocodiles to be their brothers, and hence to be venerated like all their ancestors. At regular intervals, they sacrifice a cow in commemoration, cutting it up in pieces and placing them along the lake shores. Then, chanting, dancing and clapping their hands, they entice the crocodiles to come out of the waters to enjoy a tasty tidbit.

Perhaps there really is something to the idea that they're all one happy family: the locals insist that never, ever have any of the local fishermen been snatched by the lake crocs.

You'll find all kinds of intriguing fruit and vegetables on the market stalls.

A cruise to the neighbouring islets on any one of a variety of craft is a marvellous experience. **Nosy Tanikely** and **Nosy Komba** are the best known, the one for its coral reef enclosing a lagoon where thousands of jewelled fish will eat from your hand, and the other for its lemur reserve, where the lemurs are anything but reserved. **Nosy Sakatia** is less frequented, but it's worth the canoe trip to get there to watch the fishermen. Much further off, but equally delightful, **Nosy Iranja** (sea turtles) and **Nosy Mitsio** (tiny islets) offer unspoilt nature, limpid depths and white sand beaches.

Dining Out

Malagasy cooking is a mixture of African, Asian and French flavours. The many varieties of rice *(vary)* are the basis of a multitude of dishes which change from region to region. Meat is as plentiful on the high plateau as is fish and seafood along the coast. Food is not seasoned during cooking, but thick sauces of chilli and achar *(lasary)* are served separately so that you can spice the food to your own taste.

The classic menus of the European-style restaurants invariably include a remarkable *foie gras* as the starter, fillet of zebu as the main dish, a choice of cheese and all the exotic fruits under the sun. The whole meal should be washed down by a white wine from Betsileo or a rosé, gris or red from around Fianarantsoa.

The quality of these dishes will encourage you to taste some more unusual specialities. Try the universally available *romazava*, the delicious national dish of zebu stew mixed with *brèdes*, green vegetables and seasonings that vary according to the personal whim of the chef.

The other great Malagasy dish is *ravitoto*, made from pork and manioc leaves. Poultry dishes include chicken in coconut sauce and a tasty duck with vanilla.

Refreshing tropical fruit drinks help you to withstand the heat. Noteworthy local wines including champagne *(vatoraraka)* are cheaper than imported wine, which is often spoilt by poor storage. *Betsa betsa* is a sugar cane alcohol produced on the east coast and not to be confused with authentic rum *(toaka gasy)* produced in the main at Djamandjary on the island of Nosy Be. *Litchel*, a white rum delicately flavoured with lychees, is a delicious variant. Also good are the local beer and a quality mineral water sold as *Visy Gasy*.

Shopping

Malagasy craftsmen are universally excellent. Carved wooden souvenirs include statues and games of "solitaire", where the board is of precious wood and the marbles are various semi-precious stones.

Traditional basketwork is found everywhere and in all forms. Apart from silver bracelets, good jewellery is rare, but lengths of cotton or wild silk, particularly *lambas*, huge coloured shawls originally used as shrouds, make attractive gifts. Antaimoro paper, a parchment 85 made from bark and decorated with dried flowers, makes an intriguing souvenir, but more popular still are leather goods (belts, handbags, sandals, etc.), embroidered tablecloths and blouses. Don't forget spices, which will recall the perfumed flavours of Malagasy cooking long after you are home.

Haggling is mandatory for most purchases.

Practical Information

Climate. The east is exposed to trade winds and subject to cyclones in the hot season; 2,000 mm (79 in) of rain per year. High plateau: Mediterranean climate, average temperature 18.4°C (65°F). Rainy season from December to April, shorter in the south where the climate is dry and sunny, with cool nights.

Clothing. Light cotton clothing recommended everywhere, but take a sweater, a jacket or a windcheater for the evenings which can be cool on the high plateau.

Currency. The unit of currency is the Ariary (MGA), which is equivalent to 5 Malagasy francs (which are no longer valid but can be exchanged until end 2009). Foreign currency must be declared on arrival. Do not change large sums, but just enough for use out of town where banks are rare. The major credit cards are accepted only by large hotels, airline companies in Antananarivo, some luxury shops and a few local travel agents.

Health. As everywhere in Africa, drink only boiled or bottled water. Avoid tap water. Never swim in stagnant lakes or ponds, where you may contract bilharzia. Vaccination against hepatitis is highly recommended. Consult your doctor or pharmacist for the best anti-malarial treatment.

Language. Malagasy is the national language, spoken and understood everywhere. French is the second official language, widely understood and used in all tourist areas. Even though they have had Malagasy names since independence, most of the large cities still go by their French names.

Opening hours. Office hours are generally 8 a.m.–noon and 2 p.m.–6 p.m., but during the heat of a southern hemisphere summer they are altered to 7 a.m.–11 a.m. and 3 p.m.–6 p.m. Banks open 8 a.m.–11 a.m. and 2 p.m.–4 p.m.; they close on Saturdays and on the days preceding public holidays.

Security. In the capital, it is best to get around by taxi at night. Beware of pickpockets at the "zoma" market.

Time. GMT + 3.

The Hard Facts

Airports

The international airport of Mauritius is located 48 km (30 miles) southeast of Port Louis. It offers duty-free shopping, banking, car hire, tourist information office and postal facilities, and transport to the city by taxi. Air Mauritius operates daily flights to Rodrigues Island.

International flights to Réunion arrive at Saint-Denis. The airport is 10 km (6 miles) out of town. Car hire facilities at airport. Taxis to town are expensive; better to take the shuttle bus.

In the Seychelles, Mahé internaional airport is 10 km (6 miles) southeast from the capital Victoria. There are regular coach and taxi services to the city centre. Airport facilities include a duty-free shop, banking and car hire. Air Seychelles runs a network of flights to other islands.

The international airport of the Comoro Islands is located 25 km (16 miles) from Moroni, the capital, on Grande Comore. Taxis take you into town. There are no money exchange facilities at the airport. The other islands each have an airfield. Mayotte's airport is located on Petite Terre. Taxis take you to the boat to Grande Terre.

International flights arrive at Madagascar's capital Antananarivo. The airport is 17 km (10 miles) from the city centre. It is linked by regular bus service to the Air Madagascar office and the Hilton Hotel in town. There's also a stand-by international airport 45 km (28 miles) from the capital, at Arivonimamo, and Air Madagascar provides internal service to more than 50 airfields.

Children and babysitting

If you travel with small children, be aware of the fact that disposable nappies (diapers) are generally very expensive on the islands, and that stocks are frequently exhausted. So you are strongly advised to bring along with you a sufficient quantity to last through your visit.

For some time on your own without the children in tow, enquire at your hotel about babysitting services.

Climate

The islands are all generally hot, but they vary in rainfall and periods of respite from the heat, depending upon proximity to the equator, winds and topography.

Mauritius, Réunion, Mayotte and the Comoro Islands see their 87 coolest, driest season from May to October or November; along the coast temperatures range from 20 to 27°C, while in the interior it may drop to 15°C. The weather is hotter from December to March, this season is more remarkable for the tropical cyclones that occasionally buffet the islands, rather than the increase in heat.

The climate of the Seychelles is most pleasant from December to March.

Madagascar sees much the same weather as Mauritius and Réunion, but that is the generalized picture; in fact, the complex relief of the island and its length give it a multitude of micro-climates. The east coast is, to simplify, hot and humid, while the southwest is desert-like. It has been known for temperatures to reach 44°C on the coast and –15°C in the high central plateau (altitude up to 1,500 m), where it occasionally snows. The best months to visit are April, May and September.

Communications

In the Comoro Islands, direct dialling is available in the cities; otherwise international calls have to be placed through the operator. In the other islands you can direct-dial from your hotel or from a public phone booth, which take phone cards. You can send a fax from most hotels, which may also have internet facilities. You will also find internet cafés in the larger cities. Airmail to Europe takes one or two weeks.

Driving

Car rental services are available at the international airports of Mauritius, Réunion and the Seychelles, and there are many options as well in their major towns. Madagascar and the Comoros, on the other hand, are less well-equipped for car hire, and since there is usually a big demand for cars in high season, it's wise to make your arrangements at home, well in advance of your visit, to avoid disappointment. In some places, such as Madagascar, a four-wheel-drive vehicle is indispensable, especially in the rainy season.

The minimum age for car rental is generally 21, and you may need to produce an International Driving Licence.

The state of the roads varies from one island to another. Seychelles, Réunion, Mayotte and Mauritius have the best road networks; Mauritius drives on the left like the UK. On Madagascar and the Comoros, only the major routes have been paved; the rest are simple dirt roads.

Electricity

220/240 volts AC. Plugs vary from two round pins to three

square pins UK-style, so bring along an all-purpose adaptor.

Emergencies

Most problems can be handled at the hotel desk or, as the case may be, by your tour operator's agent on the spot. If necessary, they can appeal to the local police or get in touch with your consulate or embassy.

Essentials

For these tropical climes, lightweight, loose clothing is what you should pack, preferably in comfortable cotton. Casual styles are the rule, unless you plan to stay in a luxury hotel, where you may want something more formal. You'll need swimwear and a sunhat, too. Save your beachwear for the beach or swimming pool: in any hotel, however informal, you'll need more modest attire for mealtimes—though men are not expected to wear a tie.

It's advisable to bring along a long-sleeved lightweight jacket or cardigan for cool evenings and air-conditioned interiors. If you intend to visit the high plateaux of Madagascar or Mauritius, or climb the mountains of Réunion, you'll need warmer sweaters and jackets. Prepare for a tropical rainstorm by packing something waterproof.

Besides sandals, a comfortable pair of sturdy, flat walking shoes is indispensable for excursions to the interior, especially in Réunion and Madagascar. And it wouldn't be amiss to pack a pair of bathing shoes.

Come equipped with plenty of sun lotion, insect repellent, and if possible, a mosquito net.

Formalities

Your travel agent or embassy can advise you as to required documents, as they will vary depending on your nationality. The guidelines given below apply to Europeans and North Americans.

As a rule, personal effects such as cameras, sports equipment, binoculars, etc. may be carried in and out of the Indian Ocean islands without problem. It is recommended that you make a record of the numbers and trademarks of your cameras and lenses in advance, and if possible bring along the purchase receipts.

Passports and visas. For Mauritius, Réunion and the Seychelles, a valid passport is the only requirement for entry. In the case of Réunion, a National Identity Card will suffice for EU citizens.

Madagascar requires a passport and a visa. The 90-day visa for Madagascar may be obtained in advanced from a Malgache representation in your country, or at the airport on arrival against a 89 fee of MGA28,000. Travellers cheques may not be used.

For the Comoro Islands you need a passport, and visa for stays of more than 24 hours. The visa application form is supplied at the airport and is delivered by the Immigration Office. The fee of CFr 3,000 for 2–5 days or CFr 6,000 for 6–15 days must be paid in cash, in a freely convertible currency. You will be asked on arrival to show an onward or return air ticket, sufficient funds, and proof of accommodation.

Import restrictions. Firearms and drugs are prohibited. Fruits and vegetables, flowers, and meat products are restricted or prohibited. You cannot import duty-free perfume into Madagascar, and the import of local currency is restricted to MGA 4,000.

The chart below shows the amounts of tobacco and alcohol you may import into each island.

Export restrictions. Local bank-notes may not be exported from Madagascar nor exchanged into foreign currency. In the Seychelles, the exportation of coco-de-mer nuts and shells is restricted.

Health

Your holiday will probably go swimmingly, with no more upset than a burnt nose. But it's best to be prepared for anything, and comprehensive health insurance is emphatically recommended.

No particular vaccinations are officially required for entry into any of the islands (unless you are arriving from areas infected by yellow fever or cholera). Malaria prophylaxis, however, is recommended by Madagascar, Comoros and Mauritius. Ask your doctor for advice. The availability of medications varies from island to island, so it is best to bring along a few basics: aspirin or

Islands	Tobacco	Alcohol
Comoro Islands (persons 18 years and over)	400 cigarettes or 100 cigars or 500 g tobacco	One bottle
Madagascar (persons 21 years and over)	500 cigarettes or 25 cigars or 500 g tobacco	One bottle
Mauritius (persons 16 years and over)	200 cigarettes or 50 cigars or 250 g tobacco	1 litre spirits and 2 litres wine, ale or beer
Réunion and Mayotte (persons 17 years and over, arriving from non-EU countries)	200 cigarettes or 50 cigars or 250 g tobacco	1 litre spirits over 22% or 2 litres spirits or sparkling wines up to 22% and 2 litres non-sparkling wine
Seychelles (persons 18 years and over)	400 cigarettes or 500 g tobacco	2 litres alcoholic beverages

90

other pain relief, sore throat lozenges, a wide-spectrum antibiotic, disinfectant for wounds, diarrhoea tablets. If you regularly take a specific medication, bring an adequate supply.

The sun, mosquitoes, water and food may be the cause of some upsets for the tourist who fails to take precautions. Rule No. 1 is to screen yourself from the burning sun, especially the first days of your stay, by lavish use of a sun cream with a high coefficient of protection. During the hottest part of the day, you'll do well to wear a sunhat and a T-shirt to avoid sunstroke or at the minimum red shoulders. The tropical sun is a lot more ferocious than you may realize.

On some of the islands, mosquitoes may be carriers of malaria. But even where they are benign, their bites are a nuisance. Be generous in applying insect repellent and, for undisturbed nights, string a mosquito net around your bed.

To avoid stomach upsets, stick to bottled water, avoid salads and raw meat, and peel fruit. Beware, especially at the beginning of your stay, of spicy dishes like curries: your stomach may rebel if it's not used to such a diet.

Avoid walking barefoot on marshy terrain and swimming in lakes and rivers, where the bilharzia parasite may be lurking.

Divers and snorkellers are sometimes the victim of an ear infection, the result of bacteria or fungus. As a precaution, when you come out of the water, rinse out your ears with clean drinking water or a sterile salt solution and then dry them well. If infection should set in, keep away from the water and consult a doctor; in no case neglect it, as it could lead to a burst eardrum. Treat any scratches from underwater coral with disinfectant or antibiotic powder.

Holidays and festivals

A great variety of cultural and religious festivals are celebrated in the Indian Ocean, occasions for ceremonies and parades; other holidays commemorate historical events. All result in the closure of banks and offices. In the Comoros, restaurants close during the day during Ramadan.

Mauritius:
   January 1 and 2
   March 12 (Independence Day)
   May 1
   August 15
   November 1 (All Saints Day)
   December 25
In addition, there are several religious holidays that differ from community to community. Some of the most impressive Hindu festivals are Maha Shivaratree, Ougadi, Ganesh Chaturthi, Divali, 91

and Holi. The Chinese Dragon Festival resembles the Hong Kong celebrations.

Réunion and Mayotte celebrate the same holidays as France:
    January 1
    May 1
    Easter Monday
    July 14 (Bastille Day)
    Ascension
    November 1 (All Saints Day)
    November 11
    December 25
Réunion also celebrates various Hindu, Muslim and Chinese holidays, some of which feature spectacular ceremonies, such as the Cavadee, a Hindu festival held in February or March.

Seychelles:
    January 1 and 2
    May 1
    June 5 (Liberation Day)
    June 29 (Independence Day)
    Good Friday, Saturday and
    Easter Sunday
    Assumption
    November 1 (All Saints Day)
    Immaculate Conception Day
    December 25

Comoro Islands:
    July 6 (Independence Day)
    November 27 (Anniversary of
    Pres. Abdallah's assassination)
A number of Islamic holy days are also observed, including the beginning and end of Ramadan.

Madagascar:
    January 1
    Commemoration of the 1947
    Rebellion (March)
    Good Friday
    Easter Monday
    May 1
    Ascension, Whitsun
    Independence Day (June)
    All Saints' Day
    December 25
    Anniversary of the Republic of
    Madagascar (December)
Madagascar's most impressive ceremony is the Famadihana, during which ancestors are disinterred to "attend" the village celebration. It is a great honour for a visitor to be invited to this event.

Local transport
Come fortified with good will and patience, as the islanders generally have a relaxed attitude to time, and in some places public transport vehicles will not budge until they are filled up.

Bus services are available in Mauritius, but using them to cross the island involves many transfers, and the drivers are fearless so you need solid nerves. Taxis are plentiful but make sure you agree on the price before setting off.

Saint-Denis on Réunion has a good bus network, and to circle the island there is a comfortable coach service. Taxis abound in the larger communities on the island, gathering especially round the main hotels.

The only form of public transport available in the Comoro Islands is bush taxi. But you can hire a car or scooter.

In the Seychelles, buses operate on Mahé, Praslin and La Digue, and coaches make airport transfers and excursions. Mahé and Praslin have adequate taxi service. Ferries and other boats ply the waters from island to island; alternatively there is a plane or helicopter service.

The public bus on Madagascar charges a flat fare regardless of distance. The *taxi-brousse* is a minibus that follows a fixed route but not a fixed timetable as it only leaves from departure point when full. The *taxi-be* is smaller and quicker but more expensive; timetables are posted at the stops (which it shares with the *taxi-brousse*). There are also normal taxis, for which fares should be agreed upon in advance. You will also see rickshaws.

Media

Mauritius has several daily newspapers in French and English. Radio is programmed in English, French and Hindi.

In Réunion, the daily newspapers, television and radio programming are in French. France-Inter is re-transmitted directly by satellite.

The daily *Seychelles Today* publishes articles in English, French and Creole. Radio Seychelles broadcasts news in English at 6 p.m. daily, in French at 12.30 p.m. The television diffuses news in French at 8.30 p.m. on Friday, Saturday and Sunday.

The Comoro Islands publish a weekly newspaper in French called *L'Archipel*. Mayotte's weekly is called *L'Insulaire*. The French television channels are broadcast 24 hours late.

Madagascar publishes several dailies in French.

Pets

Surely you won't want to inflict the temperatures of the tropics on your Fido, but if that isn't reason enough to leave him at home, the health regulations will manage to discourage you. In the case of the Seychelles, cats and dogs are not admitted unless they come directly from the UK or Ireland or have spent 6 months in UK quarantine. Mauritius requires a 6-month quarantine. For the other islands, even if you show import permit, health certificate and rabies vaccination certificate, you risk a possible quarantine after sanitary inspection on arrival.

Photography

If you are still using standard film, make sure you bring a sufficient supply, and an extra battery 93 for your camera. Film is very expensive on the Indian Ocean islands. It is not always stocked in conditions to withstand the heat and humidity, and often perishes.

Pack your photo supplies in a light-coloured, soft-bodied carry-all, with the lenses in rigid cases. As wind and sand, as well as the humidity, could damage your material, wrap everything in plastic film before putting it into your photo case.

The tropical sun is burning hot, so consider bringing along a sunshade and filters for your lenses. Before you start taking your photographs, decide whether you need to compensate for the brilliant light in your settings.

It is forbidden to photograph military or police installations in Madagascar.

Restaurants

Apart from hotel restaurants, which often present "theme" buffets in the evening, the islands have a raft of dining spots featuring Creole, Chinese and Indian food. You will come away with an appreciation for the succulent local cuisine, which is generally quite spicy. The restaurants are located mainly on the coast and in the towns.

Social graces

On islands where the population is largely Muslim, such as the Comoros, modest dress should be worn in public places and religious customs respected—this means using a little circumspection about photographing the inhabitants, or smoking and eating in public during Ramadan.

A general rule for all the islands is to restrict beachwear to your resort hotel or the public beaches and not to parade in town in skimpy attire.

In Madagascar, you should respect the local taboos *(fady)* and seek local advice before approaching tombs and graves.

Safety

Although crime statistics for these islands bear no resemblance to those of the big cities of America or Africa, theft has unquestionably increased in recent years. The standard of living is much lower here than where you come from, so there's no point in putting temptation in anyone's path by bringing along expensive jewellery, luggage with prestigious labels or any other costly items. Above all, don't carry or wear anything valuable in the street, on the beach or in the back country.

The majority of hotels have safes, either at the reception desk or in the rooms, where you can deposit your valuables, passport, plane tickets, etc. Never leave valuable objects in a suitcase (even if it is locked) or in your hotel room. Nothing you would regret losing should be left in a car or excursion coach, or left unattended on the beach.

To venture into Madagascar's interior highlands, it's better to join a group tour, as bandits operate in certain areas.

Tipping

Waiters should be tipped 10 per cent whenever service has not automatically been included in the restaurant bill. Other tipping is not expected, except on Réunion where French customs predominate: service charges are usually included in restaurant and hotel bills; taxi drivers and others who provide services should also be tipped 10 per cent.

Toilets

Look for public toilets at bus stations, town markets or public beaches. If you use the facilities of a bar or restaurant, it would be polite to buy something to drink. It is prudent to carry a small supply of toilet paper at all times.

Tourist information

Mauritius Tourism Promotion Authority
11th floor, Air Mauritius Centre, John Kennedy Street, Port Louis
Tel. (+230) 210 15 45
Fax (+230) 212 51 42
www.mauritius.net

Comité du Tourisme
de la Réunion
Place du 20 Décembre 1848,
BP 615, 97472 Saint-Denis
Tel. (+33) 2 62 21 00 41
Fax (+33) 2 62 21 00 21
www.la-reunion-tourisme.com

Seychelles Tourist Board
Bel Ombre, P.O. Box 1262
Victoria, Mahé
Tel. (+248) 67 13 00
Fax (+248) 62 06 20
www.aspureasitgets.com

Comores: Direction générale
du Tourisme et de l'Hôtellerie
BP 97, Moroni
Tel. (+269) 74 42 42
Fax (+269) 74 42 41

Comité du Tourisme de Mayotte
BP 1169, 98846 Mayotte
Tel. (+269) 61 09 09
Fax (+269) 61 03 46
www.mayotte-tourisme.com

Madagascar:
Office national du Tourisme
3, rue Elysée
Ravelontsalama Ambatomena
BP 1780, 101 Antananarivo
Tel. (+261) 22 660 85
Fax (+261) 22 660 98
www.madagascar-tourisme.com

Weights and measures

Metric system, except in the Seychelles, where a mixture of imperial and metric systems operates. 95

INDEX

GENERAL EDITOR
  Barbara Ender-Jones
LAYOUT
  Luc Malherbe
PHOTO CREDITS
  Claude Hervé-Bazin: pp. 1, 36, 41, 43, 49, 52, 56, 59
  Frilet/hemis.fr: pp. 3, 20
  Boisberranger/hemis.fr: pp. 5, 35
  Barbier/hemis.fr: p. 38
  Gardel/hemis.fr: pp. 71, 77
  Guiziou/hemis.fr: p. 84
  CORBIS/Robert van der Hilst: p. 63
  Jean-Pierre Expert: p. 23
  Bernard Joliat: pp. 28, 79, 81
MAPS
  Elsner & Schichor;
  JPM Publications

Copyright © 2007, 1996 by JPM Publications S.A. 12, avenue Wilma-Fraisse, 1006 Lausanne, Switzerland information@jpmguides.com www.jpmguides.com/

Printed in Switzerland
Weber/Bienne (CTP) — 10244.00.0402
Edition 2007